Praise for

FIRED FOR SUCCESS

"*Fired for Success* is a truly 'smart' book because it tells you how to *think* about what you do, not just how to find a job! It's a real career shot-in-the-arm."

–Linda Gottlieb
Author of *When Smart People Fail*

"The authors have come up with some exciting new ideas for the job search, in addition to a very readable review of the basics. . . . Career coaches and outplacement professionals will find the book of particular value."

–El Burr
Senior Consultant for Intentional Change, St. Louis, MO, and past Personnel Executive for the Monsanto Company

"Comprehensive and helpful. I found many good ideas in it."

–Barbara Sher
Co-author of *Wishcraft* and *Teamworks*!

"The optimism and positive encouragement offered throughout this book supports the goal of being future oriented for persons who have lost their jobs . . . a great step beyond the many how-to books that simply lead to another job without gain in overall satisfaction."

–Ramona Howard
Vice-President at the leading outplacement firm of Drake Beam Morin, Inc.

FIRED

for

SUCCESS

FIRED

for

SUCCESS

How to Turn Losing Your Job into an Opportunity of a Lifetime

Judith A. Dubin and
Melanie R. Keveles

Illustrated by Nancy Margulies

WARNER BOOKS

A Warner Communications Company

Warner Books, Inc., 666 Fifth Avenue, New York, NY 10103

 A Warner Communications Company

Designed by Richard Oriolo
Cover illustration by Joel Cadman
Cover design by Eileen Kramer

Printed in the United States of America
First Printing: February 1990
10 9 8 7 6 5 4 3 2 1

Library of Congress Cataloging-in-Publication Data

Dubin, Judith A.
    Fired for success / Judith A. Dubin and Melanie R. Keveles.
        p.   cm.
    ISBN 0-446-39093-3
    1. Job hunting. 2. Employees—Dismissal of.   I.   Keveles, Melanie R.
    II. Title.
HF5382.7.D83   1990   89-38253
650.14—dc20   CIP

**To my grandmother,
Godie Golde,
for her gifts to me of love and
encouragement, and who predicted
"someday you'll write books"**

—JD

**To my greatest fans,
Gary and Ross, Mom and Dad—
for their never-ending support
throughout this project**

—MK

Contents

Preface

A young boy, condemned by the experts as mute and retarded, learns to speak and blossoms into an honors student. A man suffers severe brain impairment as a result of a stroke, yet he retrains his own neurology and regains his ability to function fully. A woman learns that she will die within six months as a result of inoperative cancer, but five years later she still thrives. For some, these people are exceptions; their stories, inspirations or rare miracles.

In my work with people over the last eighteen years, I have been blessed to witness the love, the power, and the resiliency of so many individuals who have made exceptions commonplace in their lives. Whether facing catastrophic illness, family traumas, relationship difficulties, parenting doubts and confusions, or career crises, they have converted the difficult into the easy and found many gifts in what others might label as tragic. This reversing of our "fortunes" does not evolve from pie-in-the-sky wishing or frozen denial of what unfolds before our eyes; it comes from taking a second look, opening a door we might not have noticed previously, and deciding to take charge of our experience (and our lives) in concretely manageable steps.

This, then, becomes the gift of Judy Dubin and Melanie Keveles to every reader of this book. They not only help us embrace the reality of being "fired" but turn that seemingly difficult event into an opportunity of a lifetime. They are not wide-eyed optimists but seasoned professionals with uncanny insights into harnessing the whole person in the pursuit of success. And they do this with the utmost respect for each person involved, first guiding the reader through him- or herself so that each might uncover his or her own answers and then giving concrete nuts-and-bolts suggestions to maximize the reader's abilities and worth in the market-place.

Oftentimes we limit our horizons by our own tunnel vision and trip over our own judgments. Ms. Dubin and Ms. Keveles show us how we can see and do much more, and they tickle our creativity with cutting-edge stories in science, psychology, and human development, plunging us passionately into an adventure from which we arise truly "fired" for success. What makes their work unique is their grasp of the impact of beliefs and attitudes and how to make them work for us rather than against us. Who am I? What is my purpose? What turns me on? These and a host of other questions become relevant and useful aids. The intention here is to help us uncover and utilize our own unique and individual qualities. All of who we are (our skills, our fantasies, our wants) is honed into clear focus, so as we move into action, we come easily from a place of power and personal conviction.

Then, with pinpointed thoroughness, the authors guide us through traditional and not-so-traditional steps in pursuit of a successful and exciting career move. They leave no stone un-turned. With skill and ease, they open our vision to networking, successful résumé writing, separation statements, use of referrals, creating a portfolio, communicating, negotiating position and salary, and other aspects of marketing ourselves; they also share additional personal resources we can engage during our job search, such as nonlinear mind mapping, visualization, the dialogue dimension, energy chargers, total fitness, laughter, and play.

Ms. Dubin's and Ms. Keveles's comprehensive approach not only prepares the person who has been "fired," but it becomes a definitive resource as well for anyone contemplating a job or career change. The book celebrates each of us, and it celebrates an event in our lives that most others would mourn. An apparent catastrophe can be converted into an amazing opportunity and *Fired for Success* shows us how.

–Barry Neil Kaufman
Director and Founder of The Option Institute
R.D. 1, Box 174A Undermountain Road
Sheffield, Massachusetts 01257

Acknowledgments

We'd like to thank the following people who have, each in their own special way, provided us with insight, support, and friendship:

Annie Gottlieb, who was the conduit for this book's being published

Joann Davis, our editor, who believed in the project from the beginning

Ann Rittenberg, our agent, whose energy and excitement about the project made all the difference

Richard Dubin, for inventing a title that energized us and everyone else

Nancy Margulies, whose creativity, humor, and artistic ability are sprinkled throughout this book

Barry Neil Kaufman, whose Option Process transformed our lives and our work

The consummate researchers:

Cheryl Schoenhaar, who was willing to share all that she knew

Barry Singer and David Lull, who found us what we needed and more

Charlie Swartout, who had the discriminating taste to hire us and the generosity to teach us with humor and love

El Burr, who taught us about the value of alternative scenarios, and who makes himself available at a moment's notice

Barbara Marx Hubbard, whose universal vision provided us with a deeper understanding of the meaning of purpose

Belle Larson, whose belief in the book was catching, as well as the Project SOAR staff

Ramona Howard, who generously shared her professional insights

Barbara Sher, whose book *Wishcraft* provides understanding that teamwork makes all the difference

All our clients—our greatest teachers; special thanks to those who generously gave us permission to share their stories and their successes.

FIRED
for
SUCCESS

Introduction

Being fired or losing a job that has defined you for a period of time can be one of the most devastating experiences imaginable. For some people, it contributes to a temporary loss of identity. Others have compared job loss to an earthquake—being in the midst of territory that once seemed safe, predictable, and familiar but is now crumbling around you. It can be especially difficult if the loss came without warning—if there were no clues alerting you to what was coming—or if you were the only one being fired at that time. Perhaps the word *fired* itself causes distress, and though you are undoubtedly competent in a number of areas, you begin to forget what they are. You may worry what other people think about your situation.

When a person is between jobs, everyone around that person seems to be immersed in his or her work. It may seem natural to feel envious of individuals in jobs that once seemed mundane; at least the employed have structure to their lives and the appearance of security, even if their jobs aren't ones that you would otherwise desire. If you are between jobs, you may feel a bit lost and concerned about your future and probably somewhat worried about your financial stability. At worst, you may feel depressed, lose confidence in yourself, feel yourself plunging into a sense of despair about your future earning power.

Not too many years ago, being fired or out of a job was generally experienced as thoroughly humiliating. If the situation was discussed, it was often done in whispers, both by the individual who had been fired and by those talking about it. The topic was treated like a fatal disease. We are now going to encourage you to see it as merely a temporary interruption in employment and possibly the opportunity of a lifetime.

Times have definitely changed. Being fired does *not* have to be the devastating experience it once was. The constantly changing economy has contributed to job loss becoming much more commonplace. As a matter of fact, it is no longer unusual for those in hiring capacities to have experienced job loss themselves at some point in their careers. Mergers, acquisitions, divestitures, corporate restructuring due to new management, a downturn in the economy or in a specific industry, chapter 11 filing—these are some of the typical situations that have contributed to the frequency of layoffs and firings.

Mergers and acquisitions have been increasing at a feverish pitch during the last several years. According to *Fortune* magazine ("A New Era of Rapid Rise and Ruin," April 24, 1989), more than 100 of 1983's Fortune 500 have since been acquired, merged, or taken private. Of the 500 corporations included in the rankings five years ago, 143 are missing from the 1989 tally of Fortune 500 companies. By comparison, during the Fortune 500's entire first quarter century (1955–1980), only 238 companies dropped out. In other words, during the last five years the average number of companies acquired, merged, or taken private each year was approximately 29, whereas in the earlier period the average was 10 companies per year, almost a three-to-one ratio. The article further goes on to state:

> According to W. T. Grimm, a Merrill Lynch subsidiary in Schaumburg, Illinois, the value of M & A deals announced in the U.S. from 1984 through 1988 totaled $886 billion. That is almost three times the value of deals done in the previous five years. The number of transactions greater than $1 billion, those most likely to involve FORTUNE 500 companies, exploded from 36 in the earlier period to 162 in the past five years.

According to *Changing Times* magazine (June 1986), the 10 largest of the 2,543 business mergers in 1984 affected over 250,000 employees. The human displacement from these mergers and acquisitions can further be seen in what took place at TWA, as described by Carl Icahn, who was quoted in a *Newsweek* article entitled "Confessions of a Raider" (October 20, 1986):

> At TWA—to make it simple, we basically replaced all the top management. That's one of the steps we took in the first few months. We really replaced the whole 42nd floor. There's nobody there on the 42nd floor at 605 Third Avenue who was there before. Possibly there's one but I think he's leaving. And it had to be done.

If you are among those who lost your job due to a merger or acquisition, you can see you are hardly alone. According to the *New York Times* (May 1, 1988):

> Job tenure is giving way to the temporary worker: millions of people, even highly paid professionals such as engineers, are being hired with the specific understanding that they may be let go at a moment's notice.

Knowing that so many others have shared your fate may or may not be comforting. You may still be reeling from the shock and incredulousness about what has happened to you. Although we are well aware of the pain and heartache you are now experiencing or fear you may experience, we also know that there can be many happy endings.

Fired for Success is a book designed to assist you in conducting a successful job search, in creating your own happy ending. We maintain that losing your job is not the end of your career, it is simply a new beginning, a new opportunity. It could be the beginning of an odyssey to find work that really suits you. People whose work incorporates their skills, interests, mission, and personal vision are often more satisfied and more successful than others who may be just doing a job.

We have had considerable experience coaching individuals like you through a job search. We opened our business, Career Dimensions, Inc., in St. Louis, Missouri, in 1984 to provide personalized transition support to fired individuals. Through this business as well as other outplacement and career development settings we have worked in since 1976, we have helped thousands of individuals and groups from companies of all sizes, ranging from large and small corporate settings, to government settings, to academia, to not-for-profits, to start-ups.

We have worked with senior and middle management, professionals from all segments of the work world, as well as many non-college-educated people. Many of our clients have allowed us to share their stories with you throughout the pages of this book (with names and often industries changed in order to preserve anonymity).

After working side by side as consultants in our St. Louis–based outplacement company, we discovered that we had a special ability to help our clients identify and capture career possibilities and jobs that enable them to utilize their unique dimensions. Outplacement, if you are not familiar with the term, is a consulting field that really came of age in the 1980s. Outplacement is a process designed to assist fired individuals to master skills that can help them find another job. Outplacement consulting organizations are paid by the company doing the firing to provide very individualized psychological, analytical, and technical support during the transition period between jobs.

Because of our unique approach to helping individuals incorporate as much of who they are into their job searches, we formed

Career Dimensions, Inc., to enable us to do this as effectively as possible. We wrote a job-search manual for our clients that was so well received we were encouraged to seek a publisher and enable others to encounter our energy and enthusiasm and approach to becoming happily reemployed. That manual was the basis for the book you now hold in your hands.

Our work is special to us because it allows us to invoke our passion for helping people reach their full potential. To do that, we reach outside traditional topics of career development and job searching to incorporate relevant information about recent brain research, learning styles, wellness, and the impact of beliefs on dealing with crises. As with our clients, we will share with you ideas, information, techniques, and true accounts of others' experiences to enable you to approach your search with optimism, belief in yourself, creativity, energy, and a bone-deep understanding about the process of an outstanding job search.

With our experience in helping others like you, we do not believe your transition period need be traumatic. With assistance in "reframing," or finding ways to think positively about a situation that seems to be very negative, you can minimize your sense of panic and anxiety. You can learn to shift your focus and create new ways of looking at your situation. You can become comfortable discussing your job-transition period positively and honestly. We'll show you how throughout this book.

Believe it or not, many of our clients have told us that being fired may have been the best thing that ever happened to them. When they looked back on what the job search did for them—as difficult as this might be for you to believe—they were grateful. Often they felt empowered. They had new ideas about their marketability. They had expanded their horizons. They had investigated opportunities different from those they had previously considered possible. They had learned how to do an outstanding job search.

Take, as an example, the fifty-eight-year-old human resources director who was fired because his company needed to drastically decrease overhead just to stay alive. It was the second time in three years that he had found himself working for an ailing company and eventually being fired. After our counseling, he ended up in a profitable company, at a job that drew on more of his talents than previous jobs had, and at a significantly higher salary. He is grateful that he was forced to change jobs because his new job has significantly greater management responsibility and more opportunity for personal growth.

Or the fifty-two-year-old administrator who was fired after he spent twenty years of his life developing support services for his city and is now making a living at a beloved avocation as a director of philanthropy for a foundation. He told us that he is grateful for a process that allowed him to expand and stretch himself.

Or the thirty-eight-year-old woman who was a claims adjuster in an insurance agency and ended up as a risk manager in a corporation. She is grateful for discovering a new fit for her skills, one she would not have believed possible. Asked in mid–job search, when her finances were dwindling along with her self-confidence, "Would you like your former job back?" she answered with a resounding "No, I wouldn't go back there for a million dollars. I've got options now which I didn't know were possible."

Accordingly, our goal is to have you beginning to feel positive, hopeful, and to have you working yourself toward your next position by the time you finish the last page of this book—by applying our suggestions.

Fired for Success has been written to be your personal guide through the process of finding your next position and to expand your awareness of what your possibilities are. It is designed to be read and savored from the beginning rather than glanced through for a few job-search tips. We hope to make a contribution to your sense of who you are and what you can be, to assist you in uncovering what makes *you* unique.

Rather than giving you a set of skills and behaviors, our focus is on what you are thinking and feeling—on your mind-set. Effective job searches result from clarity of mind and elimination of fear and self-doubt.

We choose to look at the event of losing one's job as an opportunity, rather than a catastrophe. True, you probably would not have chosen to lose your job. Even if you had been contemplating leaving, you would rather be making the decision than having it made for you. But now that you have had to leave, it can be more effective to consciously choose to focus on what you are moving toward, rather than what you are moving away from.

Before you begin *Fired for Success,* you ought to know that we stand apart from many conventional approaches.

- The typical job-search book suggests that you send out large numbers of résumés. We focus on the importance of your searching out your unmet needs and being very discriminating about how you use résumés.

- Other job-search books suggest that you look for a job that is similar to the job you just left. We look closely at what worked for you in your last job and what did not—resulting in the consideration of many new options.

- Other job-search books urge you to write your résumé immediately, then begin your search. Our methods regards the résumé as the outcome of the process we will describe in this book.

- Other job-search books attempt to prepare you for an interview by listing questions the interviewer may ask you and having you practice tailored responses. We object to telling people who have had clear success how to act in interviews. We believe that if you are authentic and clear, the rest will follow naturally. Additionally, we encourage you to find a way to share responsibility for all your interviews, to ensure that the interviewer has an opportunity to know you in as short a period of time as possible. Many interviewers, particularly those who are not in personnel positions, admit they are not always sure what questions to ask or how to sift out what is important when they are interviewing. In addition, they may be distracted, tired, or bored with the interviewing process. We will help you wake them up.

- We will urge you to search for ways to demonstrate during the interview process how you think and problem-solve rather than just recite your past accomplishments, which can be boring for both you and the interviewer.

Fired for Success starts from the premise that people are smart and know about themselves, and if given assistance, they have all the answers.

Fired for Success is not only a "how-to" book but a "how-it-has-been-done" book, replete with true stories of clients with whom we have worked. The section on résumé writing is called "Come Meet Our Friends" and is a description of what thinking goes into the evolution of a résumé. Armed with knowledge of the process of résumé development, you will not be tempted to adapt someone else's résumé or lift parts of it for your own.

Fired for Success is designed to remove barriers. Everyone has good reasons why they cannot do what they want to do, especially those who have been fired or are conducting a job search while unemployed. We'll give you reason to believe that you have the power to minimize and eliminate the barriers to your success.

This book is for you if you:

- have been fired and have not not been provided with outplacement support.
- have been fired and have been through an outplacement seminar but want additional ideas and help.
- are currently working with an outplacement company but want detailed stories, examples, and motivation to spur you on.
- are employed but are either planning or conducting a job search—the principles are the same for you.
- are fearful that the ax will fall soon because of industry or company rumblings about imminent changes.
- are arming yourself with the knowledge and capability of planning for a job/career change—taking charge so that you will not be caught unprepared.

As you page through the book, you'll notice drawings by the inimitable artist and futurist Nancy Margulies. The humor she so magnificently reflects through her creative drawings reflects our personal, deeply held belief in the possibilities that await you.

1

A New Dimensional View
Your Mental Set for the Job Search Ahead

There is a firmly entrenched belief in our society that the only way to get a job is to look for it while you are still employed. If this were so, it would certainly put dislocated, dismissed, or fired individuals at a decided disadvantage. The truth is that employed people often make poor job searchers because they are fulfilling the responsibilities of their jobs and have little time or energy to devote to a job search—which can be a full-time job in itself!

We have had so much experience with fired people finding excellent jobs that we can easily debunk the myth that it takes a job to get a job. Of course, employed people often *seem* more desirable to potential employers because they have such high levels of confidence. They do not appear emotionally needy or anxious or "hungry," as do those who are not employed. After all, they do not have to contend with fears about financial loss or issues of self-esteem. They tend to radiate self-confidence.

The key to successful job searching when you are already unemployed is to create a mind-set that allows you to radiate self-confidence, too. This chapter is aimed at assisting you in creating that mind-set. Your family and other well-meaning associates may suggest that you need to mourn the loss of your job and go through a series of stages similar to those delineated by Elisabeth Kübler-Ross in her discussion of death and dying. However, our experience with thousands of successful job searchers who had been fired is that the person who has let go of his anger and unhappiness about having been fired is the one who conducts the best job search. Not only that, he generally ends up with a better job than the one he left. Naturally, you might initially experience emotions ranging from shock, panic, confusion, and anger, to self-doubt, self-blame, humiliation, and depression. But the faster you let go of these feelings and focus on what you are moving toward, the more productive and successful your job search will be.

If you are out of a job through no fault of your own—a general downsizing, the closing of a division, the relocation of a parent company, a downturn in your industry—you may not have initial feelings of anger and hurt, though you may blame yourself for not seeing the writing on the wall. If you are fired, however, you may tend to dwell on what you may have done wrong, how you should have anticipated what happened, what you could have done differently, whether you were treated worse than others. This can become a vicious cycle, taking up too much mental "space" and preventing you from focusing on what you are moving toward. Even though you may need to explore what happened to make sure you do not duplicate the situation and even if you have not totally resolved in your own mind whose "fault" it was or exactly what happened to contribute to your demise, it is important to move on.

You may derive some meager degree of comfort from knowing that no matter how you were fired—job-discontinued, phased out, or terminated—someone else has undoubtedly had a very similar experience. (How does that old phrase go? "Misery loves company"?) The firing process is invariably handled ineptly by individuals who are anxious about their role in it. They may want to get the firing over with as fast as possible in order to decrease their own discomfort. They may have been advised by in-house legal counsel to keep the conversation short and to the point, thus preventing you from getting a clear sense of what happened. Most often, they have received no training or guidance in how to handle this process effectively.

No matter how you were fired—it couldn't have been any more dehumanizing than what Hollywood films have portrayed of this occurrence over the years. So if you think *you* were handled poorly, read on.

In *Survivors,* starring Robin Williams and Walter Matthau, an unsuspecting individual is called into a conference room for an important consultation. He jovially enters the conference room, only to find himself face-to-face with a parrot, who says, "Good morning. You have been a valuable asset to this company, so this is not easy for me to say. You're fired!"

Robin Williams, the actor playing the unsuspecting employee, replies, "I just got fired by a parrot. I didn't know the old guy had a sense of humor. A bird can't fire me. I'm upper management!"

To make matters worse, as Robin Williams stumbles out of the conference room in disbelief, he is confronted by the receptionist, who points a revolver at him to emphasize the seriousness of the situation.

We have heard about another film in which an unsuspecting individual is ushered into a conference room equipped with a video recorder. When he turns it on as instructed, he finds himself confronted with a video image of the company president, who thanks the individual for his fine contribution and service but says that it is necessary now to fire him—and wishes him luck.

Head Office is yet another of the numerous Hollywood films and television shows depicting firings or the aftermaths of firings. In this one, Danny DeVito encounters moving men who are taking the

furniture out of his office. When DeVito inquires what is going on, he is told, "Someone said he [the office's occupant] died."

Through these satirical views of the firing process, filmmakers address the complexity of emotions involved in carrying out such a decision. Train a parrot to say "You're fired," and that takes care of it. Deliver the message on videotape, and you won't have to deal with any response. Even keep a gun handy to prevent some uncooperative fired person from reentering his former place of employment. These approaches all reflect the fear, discomfort, and anxiety in the minds of those involved in the firing process. It is too scary to deal with it humanely—too close for comfort, too close to what could happen to them.

Obviously, none of these rationalizations excuses those who

handle firing ineptly. In the best of worlds, individuals about to be fired would never be surprised; they would have received so much clear information about their performance that they would know their job was in jeopardy. Yet clients describe their feelings at the moment of being fired as comparable to having bricks dropped on their heads—the shock is sometimes so sudden and unexpected. Clients who have been fired have told us bizarre stories that are not so far removed from the tattletale parrot.

One of our clients who is blessed with a positive attitude and persistent good cheer told us he was working at his hotel room desk one evening when the telephone rang. He answered it to the voice of his boss on the other end. "Sam," said his boss, "I've got good news and bad news. Which do you want first?" Sam asked for the good news first. To which his boss replied, "The good news is that you will receive outplacement and severance until you find another job. The bad news is that you are fired!"

Next to Sam's experience, what you experienced was probably tame. If you are like most of our clients, you were called in, perhaps unsuspectingly, and told your job was being discontinued or you were being fired. Then you were probably given some reasons why, a description of your benefits, and sent on your way. If you were lucky enough to be provided with outplacement support, you would have been met by an outplacement counselor in another office at the moment of your firing. This counselor would help you deal with your emotions at that time, help you plan how to tell your family, and get you started on thinking about the job search.

Even though the person doing the firing may want you to disappear and fade into the sunset, we will suggest to you that a little later on in the process you personally telephone all fellow employees with whom you had good relationships and explain what happened. Each of them will want to hear from you—to know that you will be okay and to help you in any way they can. And you will feel better reconnecting with them and setting the record straight.

In an ideal world no one would be fired or discontinued without warning. We would all have unemployment insurance to help us make a comfortable transition from one job to another or one career path to another. Companies would have a commitment to help employees discover and develop new talents, even when they are not succeeding in current assignments. Companies would take responsibility for finding alternative career paths for employees—or encourage them to explore outside alternatives in different areas without fear of losing their jobs.

Until such fantasies are a reality, those of us who are fired need to be able to reframe the experience, to find ways to view what seems at first like a crisis—a catastrophe—as an opportunity. We need to put it in perspective—and yes, even to laugh about it. (When you are feeling low, just think of the parrot.) And then we need to get on with the task of finding a new opportunity.

Barry Neil Kaufman, author of *Son-Rise* (Warner, 1977) and *To*

Love Is to Be Happy With (Fawcett, 1977) and teacher of the Option Process, a Socratic dialogue method that enables people to identify the beliefs that are fueling their unhappiness, suggests we all learned how to be unhappy as a way to take care of ourselves. When we were babies, our parents interpreted our crying as unhappiness, when all we were communicating was that our diapers were wet or we were hungry, tired, cold, or hot. Later, when we were toddlers and had tantrums, our parents gave us that cookie we were asking for. And voilà, we learned that being unhappy gets us what we want! Unfortunately, most of us carry this pattern of behavior into adulthood—only in less obvious ways. We continue to get unhappy when we do not get what we expect or want. Barry Kaufman believes that getting unhappy is a choice and does not have to be an automatic occurrence. Nor should it be, because getting unhappy usually does not get us what we want. It often gets us the opposite of what we want—and makes us more unhappy.

If we apply Barry Kaufman's philosophy to job searchers, it would be correct to conclude that at an unconscious level they believe that if they become unhappy enough about their job loss, they will get a job. Obviously the opposite happens, and they find themselves at a distinct disadvantage in the job search because when you are unhappy or angry, you become less appealing to other people.

Additionally, when you are unhappy or anxious, your thinking processes can be considerably diminished, and you might not be able to take full advantage of your initiative, creativity, and problem-solving abilities. You may not think as quickly or with the accuracy that comes from having a clear mind and positive emotional state. You could easily lose your competitive edge just by remaining in a state of unhappiness.

Most people who begin a job search after they've been fired begin by writing a résumé and calling around, letting people know they are out of a job and "available." We believe the best way to begin is to improve your mental set in order to do some thinking, introspection, self-analysis, and reevaluation before designing a résumé.

If you were planning to run a marathon in six months, you wouldn't wait until the last moment to prepare. You'd become physically fit through rigorous preparation and training over the course of six months. Likewise with a job search. You need to become mentally and emotionally fit in order to perform at your best throughout the search.

To allay any fears you might have about money, you may want to sit down by yourself or with your spouse to go over your finances and create a realistic budget for the coming three to six months. In the second chapter we will discuss in some detail some alternative options in the area of your financial planning.

The important thing at the outset is not to become too austere about your budget or to wipe out all of the fun in your life, because you will not improve your chances of getting the job you want this way.

A Serious Approach May Not Improve Your Chances, or The Role of Laughter and Play in the Job Search

---

Of course we know that searching for a job is serious business. After all, it is your livelihood, if not your identity, that you have lost, albeit temporarily. But we also know that an integral part of your state of mind and job-search attitude must be laughter and play. We'll tell you why.

Carl Simonton, a renowned physician and innovator in exploring how to incorporate visualization into therapy for individuals with cancer, has explored the subjects of humor and play and their relationship in his book *Getting Well Again* (Bantam Books, 1978) as well as in his public speaking engagements. Visualization is the process of creating positive mental images, of using your imagination to create in your mind what you want. A cancer patient might picture himself healthy and participating in sports—cancer free. He might visualize his cancer cells being eliminated by healthy cells. Simonton and others believe that practicing visualization can have a powerful effect on healing. Dr. Simonton's examples demonstrate the dramatic effect of our thoughts over what happens to us, the intimacy of the mind-body relationship.

Dr. Simonton related an interesting story concerning a man with a severe form of cancer who had been given an experimental drug and told it might put him into remission and could possibly eliminate his cancer. He felt extremely positive about participating in this experiment, partly because the doctors administering the drug were so positive about the possible outcome. Thankfully, he did go into remission, went home, and proceeded with his life.

One day a few months later, however, he read in the newspaper that the results of the study about the effects of this new drug, the one he had taken, were clear. It was *no longer* thought to be effective in combating cancer. The next day he returned to the emergency room with a severe relapse.

Another of Dr. Simonton's stories involved four individuals trying a new drug to treat their particular illness. The doctor administering the drug was extremely hopeful about the potential positive effects and reflected excitement about these possibilities. Three of the four individuals went into remission, an extremely high ratio.

The program was then handed over to another doctor who was nicknamed, in retrospect, Marvin Milktoast. He lacked the high energy and enthusiasm about the possible outcome of the drug on sick patients. He may have felt the same degree of hope, but he did not convey it to the patients. With the next group of individuals to take the drug, its effect was statistically insignificant—almost nonexistent.

So you see that a positive mental attitude, both on the part of the patients and their caretakers, made a tremendous difference in the outcome. And a negative attitude had a major impact also.

Simonton insists that it is important for play to be incorporated into one's life to further increase one's chances of recovery. Play, which we define as any action that produces the emotion of joy or fun, increases vital energy. And when vital energy increases, so do creativity, flexibility of thinking, shifts in perspective, and a sense of control over your own life. Laughter and play go hand in hand with having the beliefs and thoughts that will most easily propel you on a positive job search.

Norman Cousins, author of the classic *Anatomy of an Illness* (Bantam, 1983), discovered the importance of humor and light-heartedness when he checked himself into a hotel to assist in his recovery from a life-threatening illness. He found that watching Laurel and Hardy movies and old episodes of *Candid Camera* contributed to significant pain relief. He has pioneered work in the area of training doctors about the importance of how they relate to patients and has worked with patient groups in hospitals committed to utilizing laughter as an aspect of therapy.

Carl Simonton saw the same evidence in a patient who was so sick he had to be taken fishing in a wheelchair. During the time that he was fishing, an activity he loved prior to his becoming sick, as well as for two to three hours later, this patient was pain free.

Dr. Simonton states that it is impossible to communicate joy and

depression at the same time. He believes that it is necessary work to learn to play. And he believes, unequivocally, that his own best work emanates from the high energy and joy that result from play.

Now comes the rub. And that is *other* people's expectations. After all, this job-search business is pretty serious—some think even catastrophic. Well, so is cancer, and a whole lot worse in most cases. Yet, according to Simonton, the best way to recover from cancer is to incorporate play and resultant joy into one's life.

So if you are inclined to play golf or to listen to the recording of Mel Brook's 2,000-year-old man or to take time out to play with your children, and others want to know why, you can tell them that this play is *required* for the work of your job search.

Energy Drainers and
Energy Chargers

Often we will have had one or two meetings with a client and will be well on the road to helping the person develop a positive attitude about himself and the prospects for his future, when he or she will walk in the next day with shoulders drooped, head down, and visibly defeated. Those are the unmistakable signs that he may have been spending some part of the last twenty-four hours involved with an energy drainer.

Ned is a vice president of a prestigious New York bank. His neighbor's nephew, Henry, visits him one afternoon for advice regarding entering corporate public affairs after a career teaching political science at a local college. Ned represents the epitome of success in corporate America to Henry, who hopes to get some good ideas about how to connect with corporations that may need some additional help in effectively dealing with government regulatory agencies.

Instead, Ned delivers an hour's lecture to Henry about how he lacks corporate experience, that the need for government regulations experts is dwindling, and besides, Henry should stick to what he knows . . . teaching political science courses.

Henry has two choices. He can tell himself that Ned should know what he is talking about since he is such a top-level hotshot, and give up any ambition of pursuing a corporate career. Or he can realize early in the discourse that Ned represents only one person's point of view, and though Ned may have a high-level position, he does not necessarily know what is possible. Henry does not have to allow his energy to be drained by this naysayer, this energy drainer.

The best way for you to deal with people who might intentionally or inadvertently "burst your bubble" is to maintain your perspective and brush off the negatives the same way you would brush off live ashes that would otherwise burn through your clothing.

People like Ned are probably well-meaning. They may actually believe they are right and that they are helping you. What you need to remember is that they reflect their own experience and belief systems. Henry needs to continue his search until he finds someone who has made a successful transition from teaching to government relations or public affairs.

You have probably had experiences similar to the energy-draining situation just described. Yet during a career search, your tolerance for such experiences may not be as high as at other times in your life. The best way to cope with such occurrences is to become viligant about spotting them. This awareness will allow you to calmly analyze the situation, noticing the statements the other person had made and thinking through what beliefs might be fueling such statements. You can remind yourself that this is one person's view. You can create a mental set that allows you to be a detective or a reporter, gathering enough information so that you can make an informed decision.

For instance, Henry, on the basis of what Ned told him, might further investigate government regulatory problems to fortify his point of view and to increase his effectiveness when talking to other corporate people. Or he might present additional evidence of needs he could fulfill in a corporation beyond the ones he mentioned to Ned. Henry could ask Ned to explain why this transition does not seem possible and then do some hard thinking about why those barriers would not apply to him. As long as he has not "hooked" into Ned's negative mind-set, Henry can learn a great deal and gather significant information that he can put to good use at his next meeting with someone else.

In addition to the energy drain induced by contact with excessively negative people, there are other triggers you should watch out for. Becoming conscious of what things "push your buttons" can prevent you from riding an emotional roller coaster. You may hear negative information on the nightly news about the stock market going down, inflation increasing, unemployment rates going up, homelessness. Downturns in the economy tend to scare job searchers who are not employed.

You will have to make a conscious decision not to allow this general information to affect your mind-set—to get you down. Not everyone loses money when the market goes down, including the broker who receives commissions on each sale. Even if unemployment rates did go up, what that broadcast did not say was how many hundreds of thousands of jobs were *created* last year. Besides, you can plan carefully to avoid financial stresses and strains that could jeopardize your financial situation.

Ignore the statistics. Remind yourself that you just need *one* job, and you will conduct an excellent search and find yourself a position which will satisfy you both professionally and financially.

Often people find themselves most drained in the evening, when they are simply tired, and consequently they lie awake for hours focused on the direst of consequences. When your energy is low, you are less likely to be joyful and creative. Have you ever noticed how the worst circumstances of the night before generally evaporate by dawn, when you arise after a restful night?

Another way to deal with energy drain is to surround yourself with energy-charging situations. Peter, a successful lawyer, has developed over the last several years a process of surrounding himself with people and materials that spark him. He starts his morning and ends his day by reading a couple of pages from a book he has found particularly inspirational. It may be poetry, it may be prose, but in any case, what he chooses to read is written from the point of view of someone who sees the world as a benevolent, safe place. While he brushes his teeth, he turns to a radio station that plays classical music or gives upbeat reports rather than newscasts of doom and gloom.

Peter plays motivational tapes in his car or sings along to tapes of music that allow his spirit to soar. By the time he gets to his destination, he feels better than he did when he got into the car, in spite of the traffic.

Over the last few years, Peter has made a conscious effort to avoid friends and acquaintances who tend to have a gloomy outlook or complain a lot. He has observed that those he sees as successful people, who accomplish what they set out to accomplish, indulge rarely in negative thinking.

So think about your current world. Who are your energy drainers and energy chargers? How might you orchestrate your life differently in order to surround yourself with those that will fuel your fire rather than feed your fears?

Some Special Thoughts About Your Self-esteem

If you lost your job because of job performance rather than as a result of a merger or acquisition or other seemingly objective reasons, you may be vulnerable to mentally beating yourself up (if your spouse hasn't inadvertently already done so). Resist the temptation. After all, what does it accomplish to mentally beat yourself up? Not only does it get you nowhere, it gets you the opposite of what you want, putting you further from the positive, strong self-esteem that is necessary to attract future employers.

Not working, being unemployed, not bringing home a paycheck—all are negative ways of describing your situation. A more positive way to describe your situation is to think of it as "stopping out" or a time of career reevaluation—or even a sabbatical. In the academic world, professors often receive a sabbatical after six or seven years of teaching at the college level. They have that year to reevaluate their options, start new research, apply what they know, travel, create new professional bonds, or work as an exchange professor in a foreign university. When they return to their positions, they bring new energy and vision and awareness of the importance of their work. They have had time to regenerate.

Though you obviously did not choose to be between jobs, you could view this time as a time of reevaluation and regeneration—and reflect that point of view to others when you discuss your situation.

You may discover that there is something to be said for having an abundance of "nonoperational time." This was the term used by astronaut Edgar Mitchell to describe his time in the space capsule when returning from his moon mission.

Since he had no responsibilities while traveling back from the moon, Mitchell was free to look out of the space capsule and think. As he did, he saw this magnificent blue and white orb spinning out in front of him in space—the earth. He began to think about the problems we face as we all revolve around the sun on the same piece of real estate. He resolved to come back to earth to start a new organization that would be designed to bring science and spirituality together and would work to end some of the conflict we all experience as many separate nations on earth.

The idea that germinated during his "nonoperational time" in the space capsule became the inspiration behind an organization Edgar Mitchell formed in the early seventies called The Institute of Noetic Sciences. This organization is in full operation today, striving to meet the visionary goals that Edgar Mitchell has set for it as its founder.

So if you are not employed in a paying position with a corner office on the twenty-first floor, tell your friends that you are engaged in "nonoperational time." See yourself as being on a sabbatical that will allow you to work toward some new goals and find a career direction that will suit you.

Using Your Whole Brain
for a Change

Up until now our focus of creating a positive mind-set has been on ways to eliminate anxiety, incorporate play and laughter, and raise your self-esteem to optimize your chances of creating a successful job search. Now we'd like to suggest ways for you to enhance your mental abilities for all the important tasks and activities ahead of you.

All of us are potential geniuses. (What a time to tell you that—right after you find yourself displaced. But it's important to know how brilliant you are so that you can effectively market yourself to your next employer!) As a matter of fact Tony Buzan, author of many books on the brain, including *Make the Most of Your Mind* (Linden Press, 1984) and *Use Both Sides of Your Brain* (E. P. Dutton, 1983), teaches a seminar to corporate executives on becoming an everyday genius.

What scientists have learned in the last fifteen years about the brain is startling—and provides more than enough evidence to prove that none of us has even begun to tap into our true potential. (Estimates are that we each use less than .1 percent of our brain capacity.) The human brain is the most complex and powerful information processor known to man. Your brain can carry on a thousand different functions simultaneously, continually cross-referencing and integrating new information. The storage capacity of your brain is sufficient to record a thousand new bits of information every second from birth to old age and have room to spare. You have more than 100 billion neurons (brain cells) in your brain, *each* of which is connected to a thousand other neurons. Your brain is so infinite in its potential that it is at least fourteen hundred times more complex than the global telephone system.

You may be familiar with research about left- and right-brain dominance. The phenomenon was initially discovered in the early 1960s by Roger Sperry, working with individuals who, due to epilepsy, had their brain hemispheres severed to decrease the severity of the symptoms. Sperry described the left side of the brain as dealing with language, logic, and time. The left side prefers linear, clear thought and excels in reading, writing, and arithmetic. The right side of the brain is nonverbal and has a visual, perceptual, and spatial orientation. It searches for patterns and allows you to be intuitive, emotional, and to appreciate music and art.

Though it is believed that the left and right sides of your brain work together on creative endeavors in an interdependent way, it may be helpful for you to think about the sides of your brain separately for a moment in order to facilitate your job search. There are some easy keys to unlocking the potential of your whole brain, so that the left and right sides can work effectively together and allow you to be highly creative. One key is music, and another is physical activity.

George was a highly successful vice president of marketing for a large southeastern company that had been bought out by a conglomerate less than a decade ago. Since the buyout, the company had been skidding, and in an effort to balance the books, George had to be released, along with a sizable layer of subordinates.

Yet even in the midst of George's job search, which included a look at filling a similar marketing position in another corporation as well as a serious investigation of how he could launch his own consulting organization, he maintained a number of behaviors that he had long since found contributed to his creative juices and success—to maximize the use of his whole brain.

First, he flipped on a radio tuned to a classical station as automatically as he turned on the lights in his office. George had not seen the brain research that suggests that having classical music in the background engages the right side of the brain. Yet instinctively he knew that this was helpful to him. In effect, classical music is actually one key to turning on the right brain. George always found that all of his activities in his office, or at home for that matter, were enhanced whenever he had his background music on. His thoughts flowed more easily and were of better quality when he played baroque music in the background. The music also had a positive impact on his letter writing, telephone conversations, and long-range planning.

George also had learned another technique at a week-long seminar he had attended in Florida. This seminar, which was conducted by a management consultant who had run these programs for twenty years, was patterned after the same technique employed by ancient Greek philosophers such as Plato and Socrates. The seminar week consisted of a number of brainstorming sessions. But more importantly, it included "walk-and-talk" sessions, three or more of them daily.

During these walk-and-talk sessions, small groups of people would walk the grounds together to discuss some of the ideas that had emerged during the brainstorming sessions. George had observed how much more efficiently his mind worked during these outdoor jaunts. He was giving his brain an opportunity to oxygenate in order for it to work efficiently and synthesize what he had learned and explored. Since the brain uses 20 percent of our oxygen intake (although it only weighs three and a half pounds), exercise and physical movement are crucial.

Now in his job search, George went on a daily walk, enjoying the springlike weather and carrying dictating equipment with him, composing letters as he ventured outdoors. When he was not talking into his recorder, he was thinking. Who would he be meeting with that day? What was his agenda? He always felt calm, refreshed, and creative after his walks.

If George were to have read the research literature, he would have been able to see how music and physical activity activated the brain—and facilitated increased creativity. He was engaging both sides of his brain and thus promoting creativity whenever he participated in a walk-and-talk session.

The Benefits of Using Creative Visualization

One way of using your whole brain is through imaging, or creative visualization. This is a technique that athletes have been using successfully for years to enhance and improve their performance. In order to demonstrate what it is and how it works, we'll give you the example of one of our former clients.

Forty-five-year-old John, who had previously been working for a major airline, had no trouble deciding what he wanted. After a three-month job search, during which he had explored more than five or six alternative directions, including a duplication of the job he had had (which had been eliminated), he had finally determined that he wanted, above all else, to start his own business. This management consulting idea was not unlike his last job. It would be the best shot he would ever have at being his own boss. After all, the greatest insight he had had about himself during his exploration was that he valued his own freedom.

Now he was facing us, sharing his excitement and carefully thought-out plans for building his own business. We were both highly impressed with the extensive research John had poured into connecting with others who were engaged in the very business he was contemplating beginning.

He had obviously spent much time, effort, and money in gathering diverse real-life pictures of how others had managed and were continuing to manage their businesses. Unspoken was the observation that John had poured all of his energy into this project to the neglect of all the other scenarios we had brainstormed together. Since we trust the individuals we work with and believe, as Barry Kaufman believes, that each of us is our own best expert, we trusted that this was what he needed to do at this time.

On this day John was telling us that he believed that an additional two months of severance from his former employer would solidify his feelings of security in starting his new venture. His former employer had previously hinted that he might consider extending the severance. Now was the time to see if this was possible.

As we talked over the strategy for the impending meeting with John's former boss, we decided that the best preparation for the meeting would include both a role-play, to approximate as closely as possible the upcoming dialogue, and John's continuous positive visualization of his former employer agreeing to the additional severance.

The role-play allowed John the opportunity to rehearse as carefully as possible what he wanted to say in the meeting. The visualization was a dress rehearsal in John's imagination, to be played out over and over again in his mind's eye prior to the actual event.

John was more than happy to act out the role-play. He could easily see how the rehearsal would provide valuable assistance to his success in the interview. His reaction to the suggestion of imaging or visualizing the experience, however, was that it sounded "awfully corny." But since he wanted a positive outcome more than anything else, he was willing to try doing it.

At our suggestion, John vividly pictured the former boss in great detail, as he imagined him sitting across the desk from him on the fateful day. His inner eyesight noted the clothing the man was wearing. He involved his other senses also as much as possible in this visualization. He registered the pitch, tone, and volume of the imaginary voice of the other man. He smelled the office fragrances of coffee, cigarette smoke, and business machine chemicals. He felt the leather of the chair in which he would be sitting.

Most importantly, John imagined his former boss acquiescing to his severance request. He watched him shake his head in agreement. He heard him say he thought it should be possible. He saw the man smiling as they shook hands to end the meeting and felt the positive feelings that this agreeable situation engendered in him.

He played this positive picture over and over again in his mind during the next few days leading up to the meeting. No one was surprised when John did get his request fulfilled.

You, like John, might think that visualization is corny. But if you think about it, many of us are generally experts at a different sort of visualization and don't even realize it—negative visualization. We often picture the worst-case scenario over and over again in our minds and manage to successfully scare ourselves half to death.

Just think about the enormous effect that positive visualization could have on your readiness for meetings and on your general sense of expectancy. You will radiate a positive attitude and build rapport more easily than if you allow yourself to negatively visualize.

If John had engaged in negative visualization, each time he pictured his former boss saying no, he probably would have unconsciously raised his blood pressure and pulse rate. Not feeling particularly good about the imagined results, he would have demonstrated his negative emotions in his facial expression and his overall demeanor. Since none of us who are feeling low ever present an appealing posture to others, after a few days of viewing and reviewing this negative picture in his head, John might present a less-than-appealing demeanor during the important meeting.

Even if John were to try to cover up his true feelings (of fear) in front of the former boss, his boss would probably have sensed John's true feelings. Since the decision to grant extended severance was at best a subjective judgment call, the employer may have unconsciously been swayed against facilitating the additional funds.

On the other hand, consider the positive effects of a positive visualization. As John reviewed the best-case scenario over and over again, he likely raised his feelings of optimism about the outcome. By the time he made it to the actual meeting, the good feelings and the ensuing days of peace and relaxation no doubt resulted in positive effects, which increased the likelihood of looking and acting like he had it all together. This gave the important impression that the decision maker would not be throwing good money after bad, that this would be a good investment for his company to make in this person's successful transition process.

Good examples of how to set up a visualization for yourself can be found in such books as *Creative Visualization* (Bantam Books, 1978) by Shakti Gawain or *Awakening Intuition* (Anchor Books, 1979) by Frances Vaughn. You might want to have a friend walk you through a visualization or tape-record some suggestions for yourself and then play them while you are in a relaxed state.

The following circumstances would be ideal opportunities for using visualization in the coming job search ahead (this is by no means a complete list):

- Visualizing a positive interview.
- Picturing a phone conversation (warm call) as going the way you would like it to go.
- Visualizing a day in your future work life/leisure life.
- Allowing yourself to picture the geographical surroundings in which you would prefer to locate.
- Telling your spouse or family about the job you have just accepted, with enthusiasm and excitement.

Physical and
Mental Fitness

One last area must be discussed before you are mentally ready to begin looking at the elements that are involved in a well-planned job search: your physical fitness. Perhaps you did not expect this area to be discussed in relation to finding a new job or career direction. However, in our experience in working with our clients, as well as in our own personal lives, we are becoming more and more convinced of the importance of keeping physically fit. (Of course, before making any changes to your diet or your physical activity, you'll want to check with your doctor, especially if you're over that magical age of forty.)

Jane Brody, *New York Times* columnist and author of several best-selling books on health and nutrition, suggests that while we may have gained technologically, our grandparents and those of earlier generations actually had aspects of their diets that were better than ours, in addition to their being more physically fit.

Jane Brody says that since 1900, Americans have had an increase of 32 percent more fat and 52 percent more sugar in their diets, while we are now eating two to four times too much protein. She characterizes this as nutritional bankruptcy. While she seems to agree with Art Buchwald, humorist and columnist, that diet is a word that comes from its root to die and that diet is the "rhythm method of girth control," Jane Brody suggests that a sensible, gradual switch to a diet low in fat and sugar and high in complex carbohydrates would enable a person to lead a healthier, more productive life.

At the same time, Jane Brody promotes the benefits of a daily program of activity that would raise the heart beat and oxygenate the body. This, of course, is aerobic exercise and includes such activities as jogging, walking, bicycle riding (on stationary bikes as well as outdoors), swimming, cross-country skiing, jumping rope, aerobic dance, and racquetball.

According to Jane Brody, as well as many others who are highly vocal about the need for Americans to become physically fit, there are many important benefits to incorporating at least thirty minutes of aerobic activity into one's schedule daily. These include an improved physical appearance as all those bulges begin to tighten up. We don't have to tell you that an improvement in your appearance will be helpful to you as you make the rounds of your job search. Employers, like many others in our society, are prejudiced in favor of individuals who seem physically fit.

Continuous aerobic exercise has been known to slow down the aging process, providing the "oil," so to speak, that makes the joints move more easily and efficiently. Not only do people who exercise regularly look younger than their "couch potato" counterparts, but physically fit people experience fewer minor aches and pains. (Melanie was exercising regularly a good six months before she realized that the periodic upper back and neck aches she had experienced for years had magically disappeared.)

Increased fitness also increases mental acuity. It's logical. The brain gets more oxygen, allowing it to work more effectively and efficiently. Some researchers are now suggesting that the slow-down of memory and thinking that has often been attributed to the aging process actually has more to do with lack of physical exercise.

People who exercise regularly experience less anxiety and depression as well as reporting better ability at falling and staying asleep at night. Aerobic exercise seems to enable the brain to release a morphinelike substance known as beta endorphins. This release, well known to distance runners and often called the "runner's high," simply makes a person feel better.

You may be like a large proportion of those people with whom we have been privileged to work. Many have been caught up in their professional life, taking a large part in creating the direction of their company, dedicating themselves to achieving, to working hard at their jobs. And many of these same individuals have neglected their physical selves, have not been involved in regular strenuous physical activity.

Yet those people who have implemented changes in their

life-style and have found time to run or play racquetball or take brisk walks several times a week report exactly the benefits Jane Brody and others have described. As a matter of fact, what surprises them the most is the fact that they seem to *find* time; their increased energy and positive psychological state contributes to their accomplishing more. In no way does the time they set aside for exercise reduce what they are capable of achieving.

We hope that you will consider implementing into your life many of the suggestions you have read about in this chapter. We have seen with all of our clients over the years that it is the subtle, intangible quality of a good mental attitude that makes the difference in the ability of people to recover from the loss of their job and find a career direction and eventually a job that is suited to them. Those who are mentally and physically prepared are ready to seriously focus on the rudiments of a good job search that are introduced in the next chapter.

2

The Reframing Dimension
Getting Your Job Search Off
to a Positive Start

Chapter 1 was devoted to helping you develop a positive outlook, a mind-set that will facilitate your job search. Chapter 2 is a continuation of the preparation and planning processes. But let's digress for a moment. Imagine that you are responsible for the production of a new marketing campaign or a transformed benefits plan, or for introducing a new product or a different manufacturing process. Obviously, after the conceptualization stage comes in-depth planning. You wouldn't dream of just jumping right in and beginning a project until you pinned down the appropriate strategies that would contribute to your success.

Well, jumping in without completing the conceptualization stages and planning process is just what many job searchers tend to do. They immediately call up everyone they know and tell them they are "available," or they run to a résumé-writing service and send out large, unfocused mailings. These impromptu activities can create barriers to a successful job search.

In order for you to produce and run an outstanding job-search campaign, there are a few critical activities and processes that will increase your chances for success. In this chapter we'll give you suggestions for stating the circumstances of your termination in a positive yet truthful manner and give you an overview of the job-search process. We'll also discuss processes you can put in place that can help you conduct an effective job search. And we'll discuss the possibility of enjoying and celebrating throughout your search. Then we'll get to chapter 3, which helps you uncover your uniqueness so that you can effectively market yourself.

Whether you have been "fired" or "job-discontinued" or "separated" or "displaced" or "asked to leave" because of a merger or acquisition that has resulted in a duplication of your job, it is important for you to move on—to reframe your situation in your own mind so that you can present an honest and appropriate story to your future employers.

If you are out of a job because of a downsizing of a division in which many people have been affected—and if you are aware of the factors that contributed to this downsizing—you are undoubtedly clear about what has happened to you. It is easy to explain. If your company headquarters is relocating, or your division is being dissolved, or the company or industry is in severe financial distress, it is easier to forthrightly describe to future employers what happened.

If, however, you are unclear about what happened, what variables contributed to your being asked to leave your company or organization, you are not alone. And even if you do understand what happened, you may, like many of those with whom we have worked, not agree with your company's reasoning, or you may feel confused or wronged. You will need help in developing a statement that honestly reflects your reason for leaving and portrays your contribution in the most positive way.

Though you may not have been told in so many words, the following is a summary of some of the actual reasons why people are fired:

- *Style differences.* You reported to a new manager who had a different management style. This may have created a dissonance in communicating with your boss.
- *Team play.* You were perceived as having an agenda not congruent with the team agenda.
- *Politics.* You did not go through necessary channels and inadvertently stepped on someone's toes.
- *New team.* The new manager wants to create his own team, bring in his own people to establish control.
- *Code of ethics.* Your behavior was not congruent with the company's code of ethics, and it is believed this adversely affected either your ability to perform or the ability of your colleagues to work with you.
- *Contribution level.* Your performance deteriorated, and you were perceived as not being productive enough.
- *Bad fit.* Your particular strengths and skills are no longer seen as a good fit with departmental needs.

- *New goals.* The company has shifted direction and priorities, and the changing emphasis has rendered your job less important or obsolete.
- *Promotion.* You were promoted and then perceived as unable to handle the level of responsibility you were given.
- *Communication style.* Your communication style is unacceptable to those in control; they now want someone more like themselves or with whom they are more comfortable.
- *Job elimination.* Your position either is being eliminated or divided up and given to one or more others who will fold your former responsibilities into their jobs.
- *Corporate culture.* You may have different values than those of the culture within which you find yourself—and create conflict with your manager. Perhaps the company believes in working nights and Saturdays, and you believe in spending that time with your family.

James Baehler, in his book titled *Book of Perks* (Holt, Rhinehart & Winston, 1984), states that if you have not been fired at least once in your career, you have probably been with your company too long and become complacent. He believes that now is a good time to evaluate your career and decide what you want to do, where you want to do it, and with whom you want to do it. He concludes his feelings about having been fired with the statement that "If you treat the firing as an opportunity, that is what it will become, and you will end up with a better job at more pay." He even suggests that you ask any executive recruiter to tell you a hundred stories of exactly that happening.

What is crucial for you to remember at this point is that you did accomplish quite a lot while you were in your job. If you were in a job eight years and received positive feedback and good performance appraisals for seven of those eight years, you obviously were productive and a highly contributing employee. Whatever happened in that eighth year that contributed to your being fired should not be given so much power in your mind that it negates the other seven years.

It might be helpful for you to imagine a time line, with each point on the line a contribution you made in your job. The point of being fired is just one small point on your time line, reflective of a situation that had become untenable to your employer. It is not, however, a reflection of a *general* level of incompetence, which is how you might feel at first.

After you have scrutinized the variables contributing to your being fired, it is important to think about how to present your reasons for leaving to future employers and to all those with whom you will meet throughout your job-search campaign. You need to develop a "separation statement" that reflects the truth as you see it, which projects you in a positive light, and with which your former employer can agree. Few employers, no matter what your reason for termination, will want to hurt your chances for finding another good job opportunity. But if a former manager is caught off guard and called for a reference without any preparation, he or she may unintentionally say something that could seriously damage your opportunities.

After you have created such a statement, you'll want to return to your former manager to discuss the statement. If you are too uncomfortable to return in person, use the telephone or do it through the mail. If you discuss what will be said about you to potential employers who may call for references, you will be in for no surprises. You can even have a positive impact on your former manager's thinking by helping him or her remember key contributions you made along the way.

Since people who have been fired usually agonize about what will be said about them to potential employers, your handling of the process in this way can save you from the worry that comes from not knowing, and then you can move on to developing a powerful job-search campaign. You may use the written "Separation Statement" in a variety of ways or not at all, but the effect of putting the words to paper usually diffuses the impact of the inevitable question "So why are you leaving [or have you left] your company?"

Developing Your
Separation Statement

What is particularly fascinating in the job-search process is that often, believe it or not, you may not even be asked why you left your former job. Being displaced is so much more common today than it was years ago that employers often make assumptions that you left because of a downsizing or merger or acquisition. Talking to displaced job searchers does not scare them as it once did, and they do not assume the worst, as they might once have done.

Whenever discussing why you left an organization, it is best to talk about what you are moving toward—in an honest way—rather than what you are moving away from. Focus the dialogue on the future, on how you are enthusiastically targeting your career, rather than on what went wrong. If necessary later on in the dialogues with a potential employer, you can tell the entire truth if pressed to do so. But by then you have made enough positive impressions that the truth will not have such a strong negative effect. And more often than not, the dialogue will never get back to the details of why you left.

Harry was a financial analyst with a large corporation and had been successful in his work in the treasury department. Since he had been there eight years, he had developed a high level of expertise in all areas of finance and had an excellent record. Unfortunately, Harry had a personality that was too abrasive for the new vice president, and was given warnings that he had better work on his communication techniques. One thing led to another, and Harry was fired. He was told that he alienated those with whom he worked, which made it impossible for him to perform his job adequately.

As Harry probed into other contributing factors of his firing, he realized that there was a new focus on decentralizing all the divisions of the company, including the treasury function. He wondered if the company would feel comfortable saying that there was a general restructuring and decentralization of the divisions, which adversely affected his position. Harry set up an appointment with his boss. The meeting was very successful in accomplishing Harry's goals. Harry made the following clear in the course of the meeting:

- What was said about him could and would have a strong impact on his employability.
- He had the foresight and control to request this meeting, and the initiative to lead it.
- He was feeling self-confident and enthusiastic about his future.
- He had some clear ideas about a different company culture that would probably better suit him.

The final separation statement (formal statement about your reasons for leaving) was somewhat different from where Harry began, but was a mutually agreeable statement. It read as follows:

Harry has been employed by XYZ Corporation for the past eight years, beginning as assistant to the manager in financial planning and moving up through the ranks to his most recent position as financial analyst. XYZ Corporation has recently acquired a new president who is decentralizing the treasury function, and there remains no position either at corporate headquarters or in any of the division levels that would allow Harry to work at the level for which he is qualified. Consequently, Harry is being given company assistance to help him relocate.

No mention was made of communication problems in the separation statement. Though Harry has no guarantee that this will be all that will be said about him when references call, it is a good solid foundation and a positive base from which to operate.

Instead of Harry's responding to his initial tendency to hide, to avoid his former manager, he became visible and established a strong beginning to his search.

Separation statements should begin with a positive statement and an overview of the contributions an individual has made, referring to initial recruitment into the company if relevant. This is followed by an explanation of the reasons for leaving, which are honest and as positively as possible reflect the reasons for termination.

In preparation for developing your own separation statement, take the time now to answer each of the following questions:

1. How did you come to join the company or organization? Were you recruited? Had you been connected in some way previously?
2. What were you recruited to do—to accomplish within your position?
3. How has your position changed between the time you joined the company and now? What has been the progression of your responsibilities?
4. Have you reported to managers other than the original manager? Was the organization restructured in any way?
5. How have the economy or changes within the industry affected your position or positions? What changes have taken place in corporate goals and strategies for doing business?
6. What have you accomplished since you have been at this company? What contributions have you made? In what areas have you succeeded in meeting your goals? What positive feedback have you received?
7. What were you told about why you are no longer with the company?
8. What might be some reasons that were not mentioned explicitly but have been implied or which you believe may have contributed to your current situation?
9. If there was a general downsizing, why were you separated from your job? Why weren't your skills and talents used elsewhere within the company?
10. How could you frame the reasons for your leaving in neutral or positive terms?
11. What are you moving toward? What are you targeting next?

12. Is the company supporting you in your transition with either severance or outplacement support? Why or why not? Have you asked for support? Why or why not?

Now you can take a stab at writing your own separation statement. You'll want to create a coherent whole out of the answers to the questions that are relevant to your situation. Rather than including *all* the details, your statement will be a clear, concise summary. Following are several additional examples of separation statements to give you more ideas on how to proceed.

PQR Organization, for whom Gary has been working for eighteen years, has been undergoing extensive reorganization due to extremely rapid growth and changes in technology. The major projects of the mechanical engineering department, of which Gary was the manager, diminished considerably as our construction programs were wound down.

Since there was no longer a need for a separate mechanical engineering department, Gary's position has been eliminated and his functions integrated into the other engineering departments. His new position as part of other engineering departments was a less than satisfactory fit. Consequently, Gary is pursuing career options elsewhere.

George has been affiliated with our consulting organization for the past ten years in leadership capacities, and for the last five years has served as director of our consulting division. His resignation was prompted by differences in management style between himself and the executive vice president. Consequently, George had decided to pursue new career opportunities which will meet his desire for continued professional growth.

Janet was recruited to be a marketing assistant for the north central region three years ago and has done a fine job of developing marketing strategies as well as strong relationships with field sales representatives. Within the past year there has been a change in management both in the company and within her department, and a decreasing emphasis on marketing. Janet is the third individual within marketing whose job has been eliminated, and we are supporting her in a job-search process.

References—How to
Protect Yourself

The first step toward reference protection is to develop a separation statement and engage in a dialogue with your previous employer as stated above. After you have discussed your recommendation for a separation statement and negotiated for changes that your former manager feels are necessary in the written statement, you can initiate a dialogue on what *else* he or she might say about you if asked. Here is where it gets tricky. Obviously you cannot ask for people to lie or be deceitful. But it *is* possible to remind them about what you did accomplish, to engage them in a conversation about your new objective or career targets, to ask for feedback to your ideas. In contrast to your most recent performance, which may have been disappointing, previous contributions may have been excellent. You can help to build a longer-term perspective on your overall skills and performance in an effort to receive a fair evaluation.

You can show your former boss your résumé (we will cover résumé development in a later section called "3-D Marketing") and even, believe it or not, ask your former boss for ideas on where your talents could be used in other companies or organizations. Now, don't laugh. We're sure you have had visions of where you would like to tell your former boss he should use his talents!

But the truth is that your former boss *wants* to see you reemployed. There is a great deal of trauma surrounding decisions to fire people, usually with considerable concern about the impact of the firing on the employee's family.

If you have been terminated because you managed others poorly and have shared with your former boss your new target *away* from directly managing people, he may be quite open to brainstorming with you. Or if you were fired from a position as manager of sales because you did not generate adequate sales through your sales people, but you now want to target development work in the not-for-profit sector, he may be open to helping you think about options.

It is possible to build bridges with former employers in this way. Even if you do not believe that someone who would fire you would be willing to help you in your job search, the very act of asking some of these questions will demonstrate your resilience and will reposition you in his mind as someone who is moving on with his life. When he thinks of you, he won't feel as guilty—and will be more apt to reflect positively on the contributions you did make.

Once you have spoken with those to whom you reported, it makes sense to talk with others with whom you may have had indirect reporting relationships, as well as with colleagues at your level and even subordinates. If you are already physically separated from your company, you can easily telephone those individuals who worked with you. You can still attend association meetings and round-table discussions. Now is not the time to disappear from sight, but rather the time to become increasingly visible.

Each of your former colleagues or managers could be a potential reference as well as part of your contact network. As a matter of fact, when people are checking references, they often proceed through an organization in an attempt to find several people who knew and worked with a former employee. It is to your advantage to have spoken with these people rather than to have disappeared into thin air. What you do not want them to say about you is something like "Oh, Harry, I wondered what happened to him. I never could figure out why the organization fired him." You would rather they say something like "Yeah, I spoke with Harry a couple of weeks ago, and he sounded great. I think there might have been a real difference in management style, but I can tell you how sharp he was in negotiating sessions with our creditors." You get the picture.

Remember: you are not a generalized failure, though you may have failed (at least in *their* mind) in your most recent situation.

Remind yourself that you have many talents and skills and have accomplished a great deal in your career. You most recently were faced with a situation that did not work out for you, for whatever reasons. And you are now on a search for an opportunity to contribute your talents and skills to someone who needs you. You are currently in search of the right fit.

Also, while you are getting your references in order, it would be an excellent idea to get in touch with key people at previous places of employment to update them on your situation. You do not necessarily need to tell them the entire story; just clue them in on what is happening now—generally, without going into the details— and what kind of a position you are targeting. They can even become an active part of your job-search network and might know of a current need in their company.

If you do take the time to speak with references from former jobs, you can be assured that they are current about you. If they are asked about your contributions, you *don't* want their reaction to be, "Let me see if I can remember. I think Bill was here two years, or was it four? And I believe he did fairly well in his internal audit position, but I don't think he was very happy in that position." What you *do* want them to say is, "Oh yes, he worked for me up until three years ago and made significant contributions to the departmental goals. We were sorry to lose him, but unfortunately we couldn't provide him with adequate career-growth opportunities."

When connecting with former managers or colleagues, it is appropriate to ask them if they would like you to remind them of what your major accomplishments were. Even in three years, the best of us forget the details. While refreshing their memories about you, you have an opportunity to remind them of what you recall as your key accomplishments, and might offer to send them an updated résumé.

Legal Questions About References

Within the last several years it has become increasingly common for companies to restrict reference giving to a bare minimum. Many major corporations refer all reference checks to the human resources department, which is then instructed to give out information only on previous job title and years of service. There is increasing concern about litigation; companies are attempting to reduce to zero any liability that could be incurred if they give out information about a former employee which is either inaccurate or could be misconstrued as defamation of character.

The reality is that the former employee would have to prove that information given out about him was untrue, said maliciously, or given to someone who did not have the right to know this information. But to play it safe, many companies have decided that it would be best not to say anything. Often this becomes company policy.

But what actually happens, even within companies with this policy, is that information is exchanged through an informal network. Usually managers will talk to people in other companies they know and trust, and would expect the same favor to be offered in return. Yet a potential employer with no inside connections to your former company may learn nothing about your previous experience if there are no informal channels to explore. Inadequate information can itself prevent you from being seriously considered for a position.

Handing Out References

Whatever you do, don't just indiscriminately hand out a list of references to a potential employer. While it makes sense for you to make such a list and to have it for easy reference, you will want to protect those references, to use them when you are being seriously considered for a particular position in which you have decided you are definitely interested. If asked for a list of references up front, at the beginning of an interview process, it would be best to try to defer that to the point when you know it is a good fit. To have your carefully chosen references called for a position that you may decide you don't even want to seriously consider is to waste their time. What you will want to do is use their names sparsely, so that when they are called, they can feel fresh, can reflect the energy and spirit about you and your work that will work in your best interests.

So what do you say when asked at the front of an interview process for a list of references? Try, "Well, of course I have a number of really strong references. I feel terrific about the relationships I have developed over the years, and if this turns out to be a good fit, I would be happy to provide you with names and numbers." Then when it is appropriate, pull out the list and hand it over. It wouldn't be a bad idea, either, if this is a new job target or a different direction for your career, to reconnect with these references before they receive a call and just update them on your activities.

If you are applying to academia, the rules are usually somewhat different. Written references are often required with an application—prior to your even being considered. Therefore, if you are applying to academia, it would make sense to accumulate recent written references, which can be photocopied and forwarded with the application. Otherwise, written references will never be as strong as verbal ones. People would rather pick up the telephone and talk directly to a reference, listening between the lines, as it were, for the energy and commitment and enthusiasm that can only be reflected in a person-to-person contact. Yet even if you are pursuing an academic staff or faculty position, you'll want to apprise your references that they may well be contacted, so that they will be on their toes if they get a phone call to verify the reference letter.

Conceptualization of the Job Search

We'd like to set the stage for you, to give you an overview of the job-search process, of the specifics that this book will describe in much greater detail. Let's start with a visualization that includes an extended metaphor for the job-search process ahead.

Picture a clear, aquamarine blue sea somewhere in the Mediterranean, perhaps off the coast of Taormina, Sicily. You are sitting in a fiberglass boat that gently cradles your body in the movements of the surrounding water. In your hand is a fishing rod, the latest sophisticated equipment that enables you to stretch your line with ease out to the middle of the sea, where the largest fish are located. You are gazing into the sea, which reflects the noonday sun in the way that it only does in the Mediterranean. It is as if the sun is having a love affair with the sea, dancing beams in a manner in which one can clearly see the bottom.

You are very relaxed, feeling very much at one with yourself, your surroundings, and your own unique presence in the world. You have taken an imaginary journey here to gain some peace and solitude, and also to think about appropriate approaches to your job search.

Slowly, as your gaze takes itself out to the middle of the sea where your line is drifting toward the bottom, you begin to realize that the waters, while still clear, are divided into four strata, stretching from the top of the ocean to the bottom. You close and open your eyes a number of times, wondering whether this strength of vision you have almost miraculously acquired will disappear. But it doesn't. So rather than fight it, you begin to put your full attention on the sea in front of you to learn the significance of the strata you are seeing.

Throughout the top strata you notice thousands upon thousands of tiny fish with rapid long tails scurrying through the water. You're drawn to their movements, and as your gaze follows them about, you begin to connect them to newspaper job advertisements, thinking

about the similarity between these seemingly disparate objects, because your mind is very much on the subject of your job search. These shiny little fish are like advertisements since they glitter near the surface and are easy to spot. But they may not be easier to catch—and are fair game for all fishermen with their lines stretched in that direction. You chuckle to yourself about how small these fish are, like the job ads that are out there for anyone to respond to—"open" to the public.

Your gaze drifts down toward the second strata of the sea, where you see slightly larger spotted and striped fish swimming in slower rhythms. How much they remind you of employment agencies and search firms. You think back on the tales you have heard from friends you know who have had experiences with these organizations. You have even developed working relationships with a few select search firms, and once got a job that was somewhat of a duplication of a previous one. It's a little difficult to convince these search firms to pay close attention to you, for just as with the job ads, you are competing with many others for these jobs. These slightly larger fish are more appealing, but a little further out of reach than the fish on the surface.

Next your eyes fall on the third strata, where there are larger fish weaving around each other, as well as seaweed drifting in their paths. How many different kinds of fish there are at this level! You cannot even begin to count the variations. To continue our analogy with your job search, you compare these fish to the jobs that could only be discovered through a series of active rounds of networking. By letting yourself gain visibility among all your former colleagues, suppliers, competitors, neighbors, relatives, friends, you would certainly hear about the jobs in your industry and elsewhere that are out there looking for someone like you to come along and claim access to them.

You remember a story you heard recently about a middle-aged man in the beverage industry who received an offer for a position that exactly matched his talents, experiences, and interests in marketing. He had heard about the opening from a person who happened to sit next to him at a marketing convention he had attended. The third strata of fish are definitely harder to see at first. They may be more difficult to catch. But the variation they offer cannot be compared to those of the first two strata. You make a mental note to attend seminars and conventions yourself when you get back to shore.

Finally, your vision penetrates the deepest level of the sea. As the unique thrill of this imaginary gift begins to dissipate enough for you to return to the job search, you notice how big and few are the fish at the bottom of the sea. Unlike the others at higher levels, the giant fish at this final level seem to take time and pleasure poking their sleek bodies throughout the coral and other rock formations in the deep. In comparison with the earlier fish, these big beauties appear as if they own the bottom sands and clearly seem to belong in their environment. These fish are more than just someone else's articulated description of a job position. They are broader, more all-encompassing. They are the composite of an organization's unmet needs and unsolved problems. They are not as easily caught because complex strategies are required, but when they are caught, they are treasured and appreciated.

You begin to think about complaints you have heard, or even expressed yourself over the years. How a president of a company wished that someone would appear who really had well-developed relationships with vendors. Or how he wished someone who had the combination of strategic consulting expertise and a chemical engineering background would appear to help build a realistic three- to five-year plan. Or how the director of new product development wished there were a more entrepreneurial approach to new product development in his company.

Employers, like the rest of us, begin new projects with the seeds of ideas that may either develop or may just hang around as nagging needs. They may be so caught up in the daily process of running the business that they never get around to necessary changes or additions which could solidify and enhance what already exists. And they could very well be losing ground by staying in the same place.

You think to yourself, as you look at this lower strata of fish, what if job searchers were to seek out employers' unmet needs and problems to solve, rather than just looking for the already articulated jobs at the surface (in the wants ads, etc.)?

Back to the deepest level of the sea, once again, and its great

*tenants, the huge fish. These fish have triggered your thoughts of
employers' unmet needs. Now your mind shifts to the job searchers'
unmet needs. Could they possibly lead to an ultimately satisfying
position?*

*You are aware that in your most recent position, you did not have
much of an opportunity to use your teaching or writing skills. You
begin to think about the job search as a detective hunt to uncover a
place where you can bring your current talents into use in a new way.*

*Well, as with all good things, your imaginary day at sea is about
to come to a close. You slowly come back to shore, and packing up
your marvelous fishing equipment and then walking across the
beach's sand, which you feel sifting through your toes, you muse about
your thoughts out on the Mediterranean.*

Sea of Jobs Demonstrated

*Imagine that each level represents a different layer of a deep sea.
Those jobs that float near the top, like fish, are most visible and most
competitively sought after by job seekers. As one approaches the bottom
layer, jobs are discovered more creatively and may approximate a
better fit for the job searcher.*

Layer 1

WANT ADS
A sample list

Director of MIS	*Marketing Manager*
Data Processing Manager	*Director/Purchasing*
Accountant	*Sales Manager*

*One is less likely to encounter jobs of a special nature or encompass-
ing a number of disciplines here. Often even job titles such as the
above are not advertised but are filled by word of mouth through
the employer's network.*

Layer 2

EMPLOYMENT AGENCIES/SEARCH FIRMS
Local searchers/Local and national searchers

Quality firms may be identified through friends and associates. These organizations are interested in filling jobs carefully specified by their client companies. People selected rarely lack the basic credentials requested. If your expertise does not fall within their guidelines, you will not be actively handled. You may be discouraged about being creative or daring in your job search approach.

Layer 3

NETWORKING TO IDENTIFY AVAILABLE JOBS

This is a preferred way to identify the hidden job market. By making yourself visible, opportunities will become apparent. You may have to make your way through a number of people before you uncover a viable lead. But as in plucking the petals on a rose, the center bud, the job opportunity, is eventually found.

Layer 4

UNMET WANTS AND NEEDS

YOURS

- creating procedures
- life-long learning
- variety
- autonomy
- travel
- control

COMPANIES

- knowledge of metal products
- contacts in metal industry
- coordinating divisions
- computerizing information
- high touch in high tech
- lateral growth in jobs where promotion is not possible

By identifying your own needs as well as those as of companies, you will be able to suggest the creation of positions even before they have surfaced as jobs within the company. If the creation of a job is seen as on a time line, you will be competing with no one else for this job because you will be entering the time line before anyone else knows it is being created. The jobs found this way will be your best fit, like custom clothing. The greatest effort put into your detective work to find these possibilities will result in maximum payoff in job fit and satisfaction.

In your job search you will be accessing all possible methods for uncovering job opportunities. You will undoubtedly read the want ads. Everybody does—even those who say they do not believe in them. But you just won't count on them, since you learn that a very small percentage of individuals, certainly less than 10 percent, will find their positions through the want ads.

You will probably find out about appropriate placement agencies and search firms, learning the difference between the two kinds of agencies and being careful to maintain a level of control over how or whether you allow them to market you. You will most certainly connect with anyone you know well, with executive recruiters you have used when hiring others, and with specialists in the particular industry in which you excel or have developed a reputation.

You may decide to do a mailing to search firms if your salary is at an appropriate level, but always be aware that this is but one of the activities in which you will engage. You might want to contact people in companies you would target, asking what search firms they use. Then you could present yourself to the search firms themselves and have them present you to the targeted company. This approach works best in corporations whose policy it is to have search firms screen potential candidates.

You will most certainly want to develop a very strong networking campaign, connecting face-to-face with as many people as you can—those you now know and those you will meet in the coming weeks. As you proceed through this book, you will learn of the power of the face-to-face meeting—and of the human touch. You will have the opportunity to develop a keen sense of what unmet needs and unsolved problems you might be equipped to address in the marketplace. You will even make friends, individuals with whom you will choose to remain in contact once happily settled into your next position. You will meet people who will enlarge your world, introduce you to new ideas, listen to yours, and offer a hand of assistance. And some day you may return the favor, since job displacement is here to stay and will probably hit each of us at least once in our careers.

You will want to become attuned to what you read and hear, responding with your own individual touch to opportunities in the marketplace. You will put together limited mailings in order to increase the number of connections you can make in any given period of time. You will commit to following up each of these mailings with a phone call and an attempt to set up a meeting. If all else fails, you will network with people on the telephone then and there.

You will also remain open to receiving information about job options and opportunities from all channels, not locking yourself into stereotypes of who might be able to open a door for you. For example, prior to reading the section on the separation statement, it might not have occurred to you that your most immediate manager could or would ever agree to assist you in your job-search process, but many do just that. You may think that other currently unemployed individuals would not be a good source of referrals for you. Not true at all—in fact, other job searchers could very well stumble upon leads that would fit perfectly with your targets though not with theirs.

In later chapters we will give you more-detailed information about the nuts and bolts of conducting a good job search. For the moment, though, let this serve as an overview, and let us continue setting the stage with further explanation about the planning process necessary for an outstanding job search.

Investing in Yourself

Among the first thoughts to occupy your mind following a termination are money concerns—how much you have, how much you owe, how much is required to continue your current standard of living. If you are reading this because you anticipate termination in the near future, you might be able to arrange for some corporate support in the form of severance and/or outplacement. Even when an individual has been gone for several weeks from a position, it has been known to happen that additional support is provided when specifically requested. If you are researching this prior to being terminated, you could present your request for assistance during the termination session.

If you are planning to ask for severance support, you should know that for companies that do provide outplacement support, the standard is one week per year of service in addition to accrued vacation.

Outplacement counseling support varies from a few sessions to full support throughout an entire job search. Chances of your receiving full support, which generally costs your former employer 15 percent of your annual compensation, are remote if you have already left your place of employment. But you might be able to negotiate for participation in a seminar given by an outplacement or career-transition company or a few sessions with a career coach who could help you get started. Even if your former employer has never before provided job-transition support, it is worth a try and sometimes yields positive results. Don't second-guess them—just devise your strategy and give it a try.

Now, prior to any actual job-search activity, would be a good time to sit down and calculate your monthly expenditures. What are your fixed costs? What are your variable costs? What do you absolutely require in order to avoid any major changes in your life-style at this point? What would you be willing to give up in the short term during this transition period, if necessary? It is really helpful to actually write all this down. Resist the temptation to just do the calculations in your head.

In doing this financial analysis, look at all potential sources of income for yourself. Include savings accounts, investments, potential earnings from a spouse or children who are not currently working or who could enhance their earnings. Though you would prefer not to tap into these sources of income, it might be necessary to do so during this transition. How could you be creative about generating more dollars during your transition? Is there a relative who might consider lending you money? Though you may not like being in a position to ask for a favor, that favorite relative who you know has a few extra dollars put away might really *want* to help you. And after all, we are just talking about a loan, not a gift.

It is important for you to do some serious thinking about your finances and develop some contingency plans. Then you will not be preoccupied with how you will pay the bills but will be able to focus on designing and implementing an excellent job search. You will be less likely to look "hungry" and more likely to be able to approach the job-search process with an attitude of confidence.

Let's suppose you truly do not have enough money to cover your costs. Generating income is an immediate problem, and the need to generate immediate dollars is preventing you from putting a good job search into place. In that case it might be necessary to look for consulting work if possible, or to work part-time just to generate the difference between what you have and what you need. One key thing to be careful about: if you do consulting or part-time work, make certain that it does not become all encompassing and dominate all of your time. If this happens, you end up in a vicious cycle that is difficult to break.

Before we leave the subject of investing in yourself, let's take a moment to talk about spending money during your job search. The well-known axiom "You have to spend money to make money" is all too true in the job search. At the front end of a job search, it may be necessary to invest in a new suit that reflects current styles and fits well, in shoes, a briefcase, and other items congruent with the level of position for which you are searching. Investing in a change in hair style at a fee that you would not normally spend might be a meager investment in comparison with the impression you will make, the confidence it will give you, and the salary you are offered.

You may also need to spend money for résumés that are word processed or typeset and printed on really good bond, for envelopes, stationery, an answering machine or a service for a few months, and a good secretarial service for letters and limited mailings if you are not skilled on a computer. If your résumé precedes you, it is crucial that it represent you, not as needy, but rather as worthy of the level of position that you are targeting. If you can get your former employer to provide these services either directly or through dollars allocated for them, terrific. If not, it would be wise to set aside adequate dollars to do so yourself. It will pay off in the long run.

Finding a Partner

If you were to be provided with full outplacement support from an outplacement company that had offices on location which you were invited to inhabit daily, you would find yourself meeting other job searchers in transition from one job to another, and even making friends in the process. Camaraderie and mutual support often evolves from the coffee breaks between marketing calls. There would always be someone in the office with whom to brainstorm, to discuss a new idea, to have proofread a letter, to help you reframe a rejection or difficult meeting, to even exchange leads.

Since you are not in a situation where you have built-in comrades, you can *create* the situation so that you protect yourself from the feeling of isolation that sometimes results from working entirely on your own. Many cities have job clubs for individuals in job transition, often through a church or synagogue. You can start by participating in one of these, but if your experience with them is neither uplifting nor productive, avoid them. Or perhaps there is someone in your neighborhood, extended family, your church or synagogue, or recently dismissed as well from the same company you came from, whom you can tap as a partner for the duration of your job search.

What we have found to be enormously effective is what we now call "partnering." In partnering you choose one person, also in a job search, with whom you meet several times a week and talk to on the telephone throughout the job-search process. (In college you may have chosen a partner to study with to assure getting through statistics or calculus or physics. In this case you choose one to help get you through this job-search transition period.) You might decide to meet in the early morning three days a week for an hour, to assist each other. With a partner you have another person to help you think through your campaign, to continually support you and remind you how wonderful you are, to assist you in thinking through how best to contact someone, what to say to generate another meeting, and any other aspect that is logical to discuss. An excellent book that offers many inspiring examples of working with a partner or several partners toward mutual goals is *Teamworks!* by Barbara Sher and Annie Gottlieb (Warner, 1989).

Creating Allies

Your first allies in your job search should be your family members, people you can talk to about all the components discussed under the partnering section. Your second ally is your partner, singled out to give you a regular time and place to explore possibilities and develop strategy.

There are many additional allies that you can develop during your job search who will assure that your experience has positive end results. And as you continue to build strong support systems, you will find yourself moving toward information that will eventually land you those offers you visualize yourself receiving.

Picture a diver poised on the diving board at the Olympics, competing for the gold. He is readying himself to dive, concentrating on doing what he has been training to do for the past several years, numerous hours every day. He is out there alone . . . or is he? Diving, after all, is not a team sport. It is one man seeking to excel in a sport for which he has been training for a long time. But in order for him to arrive at this point, to be competing, he must have had enormous support—both actual coaching support as well as financial support throughout his training period. If asked, he would never say he had done it all by himself.

And yet, people who are facing a job search often have *exactly* that attitude: they are in this alone, and they should (if they are smart and successful) be able to do this all by themselves.

Is it a sign of weakness or strength for the diver to have coaches, financial supporters, physical therapists, family members, even a fan club, all of whom cheer him on? Perhaps you have not thought about it in the context of weakness versus strength. But developing mentors and supporters and coaches is expected in the field of sports. It is equally possible to view a community of supporters—allies—as a natural, accepted approach to conducting a powerful and successful job search.

You really do not have to do this all alone. Receiving help from allies could be the difference between an inadequate job search and an immensely successful one.

Developing allies . . . What do we mean? It begins with perceiving each person with whom you come in contact as a potential ally, someone who can just as easily cheer you on as get in your way. Each new person you meet can bring excitement and spirit and new ideas into your thinking, expand your horizons, help you incorporate new ideas, assist you in presenting yourself more expansively. And each new person you meet might become a colleague or even a friend.

We talked earlier in this chapter about creating an ally in your former employer. Following discussion of and agreement to a separation statement, you could ask the following question: "Would you be willing to help me to think of opportunities elsewhere,

industries to which my skills might be transferable or people that you think I should contact?" If you have left the company through no fault of your own, the former employer is usually quite willing to assist. If you have left under less pleasant circumstances, you could still get help by asking a question like "Where do you see my major strengths, and in what way do you think I could use them?"

One manager of a supermarket was terminated because his boss felt he had demonstrated a lack of management skills. After he and his former boss hammered out a separation statement, he asked a question about his perceived strengths and ideas for possible job targets. Since his boss no longer felt responsible for him on the job, he felt very expansive toward this manager and helped him brainstorm about possibilities. His major thought was that he would be good as a manufacturer's representative. He had good relationships with vendors (whom he had not had to manage), and the manager believed he would excel in that kind of job. This opened up an entirely new area for him to consider, and one which would provide him with considerably more autonomy if he should pursue it.

Celebrate Process, Not Just Product

The celebration of process. Conducting the job search, meeting wonderful, interesting people, stretching outside your boundaries and comfort zone, allowing others to help you, creating new options for yourself, learning more about your own uniqueness—these are all part of the process, moments you can celebrate during your job search.

The celebration of process. You can share about an excellent exploratory meeting, a fabulous resource book you discovered at the university library, a particularly helpful trade magazine that you did not know existed. You can celebrate a conversation about a meeting you attended where you learned about a pending acquisition that could be important to you.

You can celebrate getting through anxiety in telephoning, having a particularly positive response from an individual you just telephoned, discovering that there are all kinds of people out there just bouncing around waiting to be met. You can celebrate your newfound excitement and enthusiasm about a possible job target or idea, discovering a magazine article that reflects your views on the computer revolution, meeting someone who believes as you do about the projections for your industry.

Celebrating process may be a new idea to you. After all, we are all conditioned to celebrate milestones—the day of our birth, our sixteenth birthday, our twenty-first birthday, getting our driver's license, graduating from college, getting our first job, getting married, buying a house, having a child, a ten-year pin for work in one company. When you win a tournament, you have proof of your skill. When you publish an article in a journal, it is concrete proof of your accomplishment. When you get a good report card, it proves you are smart. When the annual report reflects positively on the year's efforts, the stockholders are happy. When you get a salary increase, you can measure your achievement monetarily.

But celebrating process is different. Process is not nearly as quantifiable; it is rarely an end point. It takes place at midpoints (you are learning to play tennis, to juggle, to balance a checkbook, to raise a child, to build a strong marriage), and the end is often not in sight. Celebrating process is important because it allows you to be in the present, in the moment.

You may have to help those around you learn to relate to your new mind-set. They may inadvertently reflect the usual focus on the end point with questions like "So—how's it going?" (translation: "Do you have a job yet or at least some offers?") or "How many résumés did you send out so far?" (translation: "If you send out a thousand, you will undoubtedly increase your chances manyfold"). They may ask, "What did you do today?" (translation: "You should be able to see a direct cause and effect between your work today and your job offers") or "Do you have any job offers yet?" (translation: "It has already been two months, what have you been doing all of this time?").

The questioners are almost always well-meaning. They may truly care and want to demonstrate their interest. But they need help from you—help on what you would like to share, on what is involved in your job search, on how to participate with you in a meaningful way.

Since you do not have a choice about being out of work anyway, you *could* decide that your job search is a gift to you (although you would never have chosen it) and that you will celebrate personal growth, learning, meeting new people, discovering new options, visiting different companies, building friendships, and the multitude of other such moments. The job search will move faster, and you will not feel as if your life has been on hold until you get another job. When you look back on the transition time, you will have many positive memories. It will not just have been a holding period where you were waiting for something to happen.

3

Your Unique Dimensions
Your Clues for Career Direction

You are a unique person. No one like you exists in the world or ever will again. This has been proven through the process of fingerprinting that some of you may have experienced sometime in your early youth. We know through fingerprinting that the imprints of no two people are alike. Therefore we have developed an elaborate tracking system through the federal and state criminal justice agencies to identify crime suspects through their fingerprints.

Soon, as with many other procedures in our fast-changing technological climate, fingerprinting will be replaced by a more sophisticated method of recognizing individual uniqueness, genetic identification through blood sample or other bodily fluids or tissue samples. In the United States this is being called "DNA fingerprints."

This new process was the basis of a recent nonfiction book by

Joseph Wambaugh, *The Blooding* (William Morrow, 1989). Wambaugh relates the details of an actual police case in England in which blood samples were taken throughout the country in an attempt to track down a rapist/murderer. The authorities used a genetic fingerprinting process developed by an English scientist, not far from where the crime was committed.

This technology is ready to be used in the United States, where the FBI has opened its own DNA analysis unit at the FBI laboratory near Washington, D.C. Within the next several years, at least half of the states are expected to be doing their own DNA testing. The genetic material found in a small blood sample provides much stronger evidence of the uniqueness of each person than simple fingerprints do. It's one thing to agree that the patterns on one's hands could be individual, but to learn that the very structure of each person's cells is different offers compelling proof that every individual is completely unique.

Like the microscopic physical individuality among people, there are unique endowments of talents, interests, and experiences. When we look at the qualities that make each of us different—even people educated in the same school or department or working in the same job—we discover clues that are useful in suggesting career or job directions.

How often in your schooling or in your work life has anyone—teacher, parent, supervisor—sat you down to discuss your uniqueness?

In your formative years your parents were probably relieved and satisfied if your teachers said that you were "normal or above average." In your performance reviews you might have been judged according to how others in your job category had performed.

But we have learned a great deal about individual uniqueness. Some of our understanding has been trickling down to schools like the Key School in Indianapolis, Indiana, where students are given the opportunity to excel in at least seven different kinds of intelligence. There are schools based on theories of differences in learning style, where students are grouped according to their preferences in learning, such as whether they are visual, tactile, kinesthetic, or auditory learners. There are companies that administer tests like the Myers-Briggs Type Indicator, which identifies sixteen different temperament types and explores individual preferences for job activities which relate to temperament.

We still have a long way to go, because while we may have tried to treat people as "equal," we have neglected to realize fully that the paradox is that they are all unique.

Examination of your uniqueness as a preliminary to finding your next job can increase your chances of finding satisfying work. In every field from architecture to zoology, there is substantial evidence that those who enjoy their work are more successful at it and often reap greater monetary benefits. If you look inside and reacquaint yourself with what makes work and life enjoyable to you, you may have a better chance of finding a job that is suited to you.

This process can lead you to uncovering directions that you might not find otherwise. A serious consideration of your hobbies, forgotten interests, fantasies, and the environments in which you do your best work could lead you to identify multiple areas to pursue as viable job options.

Study of your unique qualities can also help you sell yourself into a job at an interview when you may be competing with many others for the same job.

As you will be selling yourself through the job-search campaign, it would be helpful for you to know as much about what you are selling as possible. Uncovering new facets of yourself can lead to new ways of promoting yourself.

Looking at your uniqueness can help combat and dissipate any residual feelings of ineffectiveness you may still have from the way in which you were fired or job-discontinued or from the messages of inadequacy that former managers gave you. And the process of learning about yourself can be very satisfying.

A sample of what happened to job searchers who participated in the process of uncovering their unique dimensions might further convince you of its merit:

- A client who had worked in the banking industry discovered her mission in the field of corporate social responsibility.
- A client with skills in marketing and promotion and interest in international travel pursued a career direction in international import/export.
- A client with an avocational interest in sports and with skills and experience in sales became a sales representative for a national line of sports equipment.
- A client whose career's high point came when he took over a failing business researched the possibilities of becoming a turnaround manager or working in mergers and acquisitions at a major corporation.

Questions to Stimulate Your
Knowledge of Your Unique Dimensions

The range of possible questions that could be asked to help you discover your uniqueness is unlimited. To stimulate your own process, we have selected the ones that we have come to rely on over the years of working with our clients.

We suggest that you read through this chapter first to get a feeling for what we are asking. We think you will also be inspired by the stories of people we have met or read about who are making unique contributions to the world. After you have read this through, you may want to go back over the questions with a partner or friend; he or she will help you formulate your answers and may think of additional questions to ask if you run into a blank wall.

1. What Skills and Abilities Do You
Have That You Like to Use?

Do you prefer to use your head or your hands? Are you a good communicator or researcher? Do you like to discover new uses for a computer program or design new training programs for employees? Are you a "numbers" person? What skills do you have that are just in their infant stages of development? What skills do you have an intuitive ability for but have not had a chance to develop yet? What environment would nurture your skills and abilities?

Profiles: Skills and Abilities

Michael Gelb, author of *Present Yourself* (Jalmar Press, 1988), combines his interest and knowledge about learning and the brain, psychology, body movement, juggling, and many other subjects whenever he conducts a presentation to large groups of people about mind mapping, a technique developed by a mentor of his and about which you will be learning more in later chapters.

Gelb is a superb communicator and presentor who has audiences eating out of his hand when he imitates Muhammad Ali to make an important point. Gelb also uses his skill in juggling as a metaphor for learning. He actually teaches people how to juggle, providing an opportunity for them to move around, be active, learn a skill that most people don't believe they can learn, and take a break during his sessions.

While there are many on the lecture circuit, few are as popular as Michael Gelb, who brings his special skills and abilities in acting and movement into his corporate presentations about "high-performance learning." No one can imitate him because his presentation style emanates deeply from his own skills, from his own special uniqueness. Gelb has combined his skills in presentation, body movement, learning methodologies, and motivating and energizing audiences to become a superb teacher and gifted presentor. Thus Michael Gelb uses his unique interests to create a wonderful career for himself.

If you were not an elementary teacher or a special education teacher, you might never have heard of Torey Hayden, author of *One Child* (Putnam, 1980), *Murphy's Boy* (Putnam, 1982), and *Just Another Kid* (Putnam, 1987). She is a gifted, energetic teacher who combines her belief in the innate abilities of children with her special skill in working with youngsters with learning disabilities and mental disturbances.

In *One Child* she describes her experience in working with a child who was temporarily placed in her classroom while waiting to be sent to a juvenile reform center. This little eight-year-old girl had been accused of murdering a boy her age when she set him afire while he was tied to a tree.

In the course of her book, Hayden describes the process she went through in finally being able to reach the little girl and gain her trust and admiration where all others had failed. This special skill in working with youngsters whom others have given up on is one that teacher Torey Hayden has and which she describes so well in her books. It's what sets her apart from others who plod along in their efforts to change the otherwise negative futures awaiting children with problems.

Are you a Torey Hayden in disguise? Do you have a special skill in believing in others, in empowering them, in drawing from them their best? Have you thought about the vast number of ways you might use such a skill in your next position? Do you want to take that skill with you and have it be a required skill—or would you rather just utilize it indirectly throughout your work?

2. What Area of Perceived Weakness Do You Have That Could Be Turned into or Viewed as an Asset?

Have you been told you are too loud, only to realize that you belong in an entrepreneurial setup rather than a conservative corporate structure? Have you been told you can't follow directions, only to realize that you should be the one determining policy or giving the directions?

Profiles: From Weakness to Strength

Barbra Streisand did not have her nose fixed; she saw no reason to cultivate the clonelike appearance so valued in the chorus. Instead, she insisted that with her Egyptian profile she looked

OR

much like Queen Nefertiti. Streisand propelled her unique looks along with her outstanding musical talent into legendary proportions and millions of dollars in the entertainment industry.

Barbara Vitale was diagnosed as brain damaged and mentally retarded as a youngster. She didn't learn to read until she was twelve years old, when she was exposed to a teacher who didn't believe the diagnosis others had previously made about her.

Today Vitale has a Ph.D. in education and is a member of Mensa, an organization for people with measured high IQs. She uses herself as an example to motivate teachers and educators not to accept the learning problems that children present to them as evidence of their lack of capability.

Author of *Unicorns Are Real* (Warner, 1986) and *Free Flight* (Jalmar, 1986), Vitale travels around the world sharing her inspiring message. She has done a careful investigation of the relationship between a child's physiology and his ability to learn, interviewing pediatricians and scientists and educators, gathering in-depth information about children's bodies, brains, and growth patterns as they affect and relate to learning.

For instance, Vitale believes, from talking with experts knowledgeable about brain growth, that the reason she was not able to read before twelve is that her brain had not myelinated yet. Myelination is a process that usually happens in children before the age of five whereby connections are made between the left and right hemispheres of the brain. Before this happens, children display problems similar to people who have had surgery to separate their brain hemispheres.

Barbara also learned that children's eyes are not always as capable of focusing as adults'. The mimeographed sheets used in elementary school classrooms are often seen as blurs by youngsters and can contribute to problems with reading. Unknowingly, teachers using mimeographed sheets for reading assignments are contributing to eye strain and a distaste for reading among youngsters whose focusing abilities are still forming.

These are just two of many pieces of evidence that Barbara

Vitale has gathered to demonstrate how we must change the educational process to fit the child, rather than expect the child to fit the process. Her one-woman campaign is a direct result of her own difficulties, of her own (perceived) weaknesses. No one speaks as eloquently or as urgently as she does about changes that need to be made in elementary and remedial education. Her skills in research and development, her tireless resourcing of experts in the physiology and methodology of learning, the pioneering of new frontiers, her ability to communicate information to individuals and groups and break all the rules have contributed to her enormous success as a teacher and trainer worldwide.

3. What Hobbies or Avocational Interests Do You Have?

What do you find yourself drawn to when you are not working? What books or magazines do you read? How do you spend your volunteer time? How would you spend your volunteer time if you had more time?

Profile: Discovering a New Career

Tim Gallwey was educated at Harvard and was leading a successful career in college administration when he decided to take a sabbatical and "drop out" for a while. He defied societal and family norms about pursuing "exhausting overachievement" and dismayed his family, especially when he decided to spend some time as a tennis coach.

Was this any way for a Harvard graduate to spend his productive years? When was he going to get back to serious work?

It was one thing for a person to pursue a sports career in professional baseball, football, or hockey. But Gallwey was not pursuing a professional career in tennis. He was coaching—and his coaching did not involve professionals. His students were merely ordinary people who were interested in improving their tennis game. Gallwey assured himself that this was just a temporary stint, before applying for a college administrative post and continuing his career.

But as time passed, he became less and less interested in returning to academia. He was learning a lot on the tennis court. In fact, he discovered that his students could learn best when he taught least. In the process, he discovered what he calls the "inner game."

The "inner game" has become a focus of a number of books Gallwey has written, including *The Inner Game of Tennis* (Bantam, 1974), *The Inner Game of Golf* (Random, 1981), *The Inner Game of Skiing* (Bantam, 1981), and *The Inner Game of Music* (Anchor/Doubleday, 1986). Today he uses his skills to consult with major corporations about ways in which companies can improve motivation, productivity, and job satisfaction.

Briefly, what Gallwey discovered on the tennis court is that in any endeavor, including tennis, people engage in an inner game— an inner dialogue with themselves that either helps them or hinders them. Imagine that our minds are composed of two aspects: self one and self two. Self one provides us with critical self-judgment, which gets in the way of our being effective, while self two is the true self, the part of ourselves that intuitively knows how to approach any endeavor.

As a result of what he learned on the tennis court coaching his students, Gallwey as corporate consultant has gone on to make a far greater contribution than he probably would have ever made in college administration. This came as a result of trusting his own instincts, focusing on the skills he had and wanted to develop further, and devoting time to a sport that had simply been an avocational interest. He is still in an educational endeavor when he works with major corporations or gives keynote speeches. But now he is involved with what matters deeply to him, sharing his personal experiences, translating what he has learned on the tennis court to the corporate arena.

4. What Were Your Childhood Fantasies About Jobs or Careers?

As a child, you probably had a number of job/work/career fantasies. Perhaps you have forgotten them, and this question will need to percolate for a while before you remember. But if you can recollect your childhood fantasies, or even fantasies about jobs or careers which you have had more recently, discuss them. Describe them as thoroughly as you can, with as much detail as you have at your fingertips.

Profile: From Fantasy to Reality

Shakti Gawain, author of *Creative Visualization* (Bantam Books, 1978) and *Living in the Light* (Whatever Publishing, Inc., 1986), offers workshops on visualization to people of all walks of life. She demonstrates in her books and her classes how people can use principles long understood by Eastern philosophers and sages—and now espoused by scientists on the cutting edge of physics—to manifest their dreams.

In *Creative Visualization* Gawain tells us (as do the new physicists) that the basic component of the universe is not matter but energy. What appears to us as solid—desks, chairs, people—on a subatomic level is really a swirling mass of energy. "Thought is a relatively fine, light form of energy and therefore very quick and easy to change. Matter is relatively dense, compact energy, and therefore slower to move and change."

According to Gawain, thought, a light form of energy, is followed by action as we bring fantasies to reality. Whenever we create something, we always create it first as an idea.

For example, if you wanted a relationship with another person, you would first imagine what it would be like to be in such a relationship. Then you would engage yourself in activities that would lead to meeting new people. You might take a class in Chinese cooking or hang out in a ski lodge or take a cruise or ask friends to introduce you to other single people. Then, if you met someone promising, you might ask her or him out for a date. The date might lead to further dates and an eventual commitment to this person. And in the course of these events, you would have brought your idea into reality.

According to Shakti Gawain, fantasies of being, whether about possible career directions or other aspects of our lives, are messages from a deeper part of ourselves that deserve serious attention. Yet how many of us were discouraged as youngsters from pursuing our dreams when we heard parents or other adults tell us (in order to protect us) that artists starve and actors and actresses wait on tables. Fantasies are very fragile—and all it takes is one person to poke a hole in a fantasy for us to instantly lose hold of it, bury it, and come back to so-called "reality."

In order to assure that fantasies do become reality, Shakti teaches a process of creative visualization that includes identifying ideas that would enhance our lives, setting down goals and objectives, and affirming our right to have what we want as long as it is of value to us and others.

Quiet, Marge. Bill's conducting a job search.

We aren't suggesting that you will completely transform your career by tapping into your fantasies. We *are* suggesting that getting back in touch with your fantasies can give you clues as to what directions you might want to include in your job search. If your fantasy were to be a media star and you have special skills in sales and marketing, you could redirect your career toward the media. This would bring you one step closer to actualizing your fantasy.

If your fantasy is to be a talk show host and you have skills in resourcing and developing new ideas, you could target the creation of a corporate video newsletter to transmit daily developments to corporations' subsidiaries. You could do the interviewing in this video production. If your fantasy is to work in music, to hang around with musicians, and you are a whiz at running companies, you could target companies in the entertainment industry and work closely with those who share your interests.

5. *What Special Vision of the World Do You Hold?*

How would you like to see the world change? What part could you play?

Profiles: Modern-Day Visionaries

Marilyn Ferguson, author of *The Aquarian Conspiracy: Personal and Social Transformation in Our Time* (J. P. Tarcher, Inc., 1980), writes about a global occurrence produced by a new vision that is held by many people and which supports life on our planet. She states that many changes are happening in education, medicine, science, and politics, and though the mainstream is not aware of them, they will completely transform life on earth.

Many of the activities that she wrote about in the late 1970s have become better known and more pervasive than they were when she first wrote her book. Marilyn Ferguson and her husband, Ray Gottlieb, are authoring a book about visionaries of our time.

Ferguson sees us as experiencing a tremendous "paradigm shift" in which ideas which once seemed valid no longer hold true. For instance, at the time that Columbus sailed to America, popular belief in Europe was that the earth was flat. The so-called "evidence" was there when one looked out on the horizon and saw the "end" of the earth. But Columbus's discovery of America caused a reevaluation of those initial assumptions. It literally turned their world upside down and made them shift their thinking.

Discussing the paradigm shift that is facing us today, Ferguson states in the *Aquarian Conspiracy:*

> The paradigm of the Aquarian Conspiracy sees humankind embedded in nature. It promotes the autonomous individual in a decentralized society. It sees us as stewards of all our resources, inner and outer. It says that we are *not* victims, not pawns, not limited by conditions or conditioning. Heirs to evolutionary riches, we are capable of imagination, invention, and experiences we have only glimpsed.

Ferguson introduces the reader to others throughout her book who are engaged in pursuits that respect life and promote cooperation, collaboration, and peace. For people who have held a vision of a better world, she exposes us to thousands of others who hold a similar vision and are actively, yet quietly, working to make it happen.

John Naisbitt and Patricia Aburdene, authors of *Re-inventing the Corporation* (Warner Books, 1985), turned their vision toward the corporation, reporting economic realities and changing personal values that will require the heads of corporations to create environments conducive to human growth.

Their book is a treatise about the factors that are inducing companies to change, with numerous inspiring tales of corporations that have already created environments in which "fun, profit, and productivity flow."

The authors contend that the coming "baby bust" on the heals of the "baby boom" will cause companies to compete for the best and the brightest workers. In doing so, corporations will have to provide employees at all levels with psychological and economic inducements from in-house health facilities to greater profit share, in addition to an increased say in how things get done.

The information age and its herald the computer are allowing greater access within the corporation as numerous management layers disappear. This enables employees to be better informed and more closely aligned to corporate policies and changes.

Naisbitt and Arburdene had originally intended to write a book about reinventing the world we live in with chapters on business, the family, the workplace, the arts, politics, education, etc. As the size of their book grew, they realized the importance of focusing exclusively on corporations. They invite the reader to accompany them on their journey as they discuss the impending changes in the way corporations worldwide will be run in the future, based on current trends and examples of successful, growing companies:

> If you have longed to create a workplace where both people and profits can flourish, you were born at the right time. And you are living among a generation of contemporaries who share your vision. It is that vision on which the success of America's corporations depends.

Have you had jobs in environments that supported your own personal vision of the way an organization should work? Do you have a vision of the way a particular industry should be moving, or is already moving? Can you imagine humane *and* cost-effective ways to enhance the human resources of an organization—ways that would be congruent with your vision of how people should be treated? Can you envision entirely new and effective ways to organize, to plan, to create, to operate, to develop, to access worldwide resources? At one time did you have a vision of the world which you have since dismissed as naive? Do you want to rekindle those visions and look for places to incorporate your talents into them?

6. What Is Your Mission or Purpose?

When did you experience intense concentration and awareness, or feelings of joy and celebration? Answer the following questions, which have been adapted from Charles Garfield's *Peak Performers: The New Heroes of American Business* (Avon Books, 1986):

- Where did it happen? Where were you?
- Were you working alone or on a team? Leader or member?
- Were you performing a service? To whom?
- Were you an innovator? Of what?
- Did you champion an idea? A product? A service?
- Who was there to witness your success?
- What activities have given you a powerful sense of purpose?
- When have you felt deeply committed to
  - –Another person?
  - –An idea, product, team?
  - –Developing a particular skill?
- Why did you feel so committed?
- What did you learn from each experience?
- What benefits remain with you?
- How did each experience feel while it was happening?

Profiles: A Sense of Purpose

Charles Garfield developed a highly absorbing interest in the concept of mission after he participated as a young mathematician in the American space program of the 1960s that culminated in placing men on the moon in 1969. Garfield was fascinated with the positive effect John F. Kennedy's mission of putting a man on the moon by the end of the decade had on capturing the energy, enthusiasm, and commitment of thousands of people employed by the space program in those years. Garfield was so enthralled and fascinated by the psychology behind this process that he went on to change careers and earned a Ph.D. in psychology.

Garfield's special perspective has evolved from studying the factors that go into creating peak performers. Aside from the space industry, he has studied peak performers in practically every human endeavor from exceptional athletes to people with exceptional ability to fight terminal illness.

Interviewing patients not expected to live, who instead went into remission, Garfield found people who said there were two factors that kept them going and gave them the will to live. One was wanting to continue relationships with people they loved, and the second was returning to work to which they were committed. Here Garfield found motivation so strong that it literally kept people alive when the odds were stacked against them.

Charles Garfield concludes from his careful research that at the core of any peak performance is a person motivated by a mission. Garfield's mission is to help each of us to find ours. He does this impressively through his books, videos, research, and compelling lectures and seminars.

In 1970, when Maggie Kuhn was sixty-five years old, she was forced to retire from the U.S. national office of the Presbyterian church. She was so furious about being seen as "over the hill" when still productive that she joined with five others who were also upset about being forced out of work. Together they formed an organization initially called Consultation of Older and Younger Adults, later nicknamed the Gray Panthers.

For almost twenty years, Maggie Kuhn has been leading the Gray Panthers in an effort to educate America and stamp out ageism in this country. Her mission has been supported by eighty thousand others, and the organization has chapters in thirty states.

The Gray Panthers have demonstrated at meetings of the American Medical Association and the National Gerontological Society. They have monitored planning commissions, zoning boards, courts, banks, and companies. They have physically "liberated" men and women from unsafe nursing homes. And they have organized ongoing local and national "media watches" to remove ageist programs and commercials from radio and television.

Now in her eighties, Maggie Kuhn keeps a busy schedule of lecturing, protesting, and testifying before Congress, state legislatures, and international bodies as the untiring spokesperson for serious social change as it relates to an aging America. She is a woman with a mission that has kept her involved for many years.

Barbara Marx Hubbard, author of *The Hunger of Eve* (Stackpole Books, 1976; republished by Island Pacific NW in 1989), is a woman with a mission to bring people on our planet into a new age. She sees our reaches into outer space as the infant steps of a people who one day will be free to roam the universe, and she is committed to doing all she can to ensure that we will meet our destiny.

As a young woman growing up in affluent Scarsdale, New York, daughter of a millionaire toy manufacturer, she constantly searched for her mission in life at a time when a woman was supposed to be satisfied being the helpmate to a man.

In *The Hunger of Eve* she relates how she questioned the young men she went out with in college:

"What's your purpose? What are you working for?" They had never thought about it. It became the great unanswered question. "How can people live and not know why they're living?" I wondered.

Several years later, following her marriage to artist Earl Hubbard and the birth of five children, Hubbard discovered her first tentative mission. Her mission was "to act as an advocate for humanity, for the possibility of meaning, values, improvement of human behavior."

As her mission matured, Hubbard took on responsible roles in the World Future Society and worked to promote the space program during the 1970s when it was in danger of losing its national support. She has played a substantial role in grass-roots peace delegations to the Soviet Union to encourage understanding between the people of the United States and the Soviet Union, hoping that the governments would eventually catch up with the foundation laid by citizen diplomats. There is evidence today that these ideas have paid off as we move toward greater nuclear disarmament agreements.

Recently, Barbara Marx Hubbard and several others founded an organization called the Global Family to foster greater peace and unity among people on this planet. She has been instrumental in forming "resonating core groups" around the world—small, local networking groups that are determined to use their resources to effect a peaceful transformation of the entire planet.

After you have answered Charles Garfield's questions on mission and allowed your responses to percolate, you may find yourself back in touch with your personal mission, which had been forgotten. Another way to think about mission is to ask yourself why you are here. What are you supposed to do while on, as Buckminster Fuller calls it, "Spaceship Earth"? What difference do you want to make? What do you want to accomplish? Do you have a mission that involves an international community, such as Barbara Marx Hubbard's? Do you want to make the world a better, fairer place as Maggie Kuhn does? Do you want to create a better world, a better work place, a better educational system, a cleaner environment, a sharing world community, a more efficient system, a more effective organization.

If you allow yourself to think about what *you* believe to be important, about why you are here, about what difference you want to make, you will be getting closer to a mission that you can use as an underlying guide during your search. Getting in touch with your mission will help you think more creatively and openly about options and possibilities for yourself.

7. What Do You Feel Passionate About?

What gets your adrenaline going? What makes you excited or angry or indignant? What generates high emotion for you? What do you really look forward to doing, to experiencing?

Profile: Following Your Bliss

Joseph Campbell has recently become a nationally recognized figure as a result of the popular PBS series in which Bill Moyers interviewed him about mythology, the subject of lifelong study for Campbell. Although Campbell died in 1987 at the age of eighty-three, he lived long enough to see his name become widely known and his books about mythology become popular.

In *An Open Life* (Larson Publications, 1988), a compilation of conversations between Joseph Campbell and Michael Toms, host of *New Dimensions Radio* (based in San Francisco), Campbell discusses the meaning of "following one's bliss":

> I'm not superstitious, but I do believe in spiritual magic, you might say. I feel that if one follows what I call one's "bliss"—the thing that really gets you deep in the gut and that you feel is your life—doors will open up. They do! They have in my life and they have in many lives that I know of.

Campbell goes on to mention a paper by the philosopher Schopenhauer called "An Apparent Intention of the Fate of the Individual," in which the author suggests that if one lives long enough, one can look back on one's life as the chapters in a Dickens novel: coincidences have meaning; seeming mistakes were the beginning of an important direction in one's life. And again from Joseph Campbell:

> If you follow your bliss, you'll have your bliss, whether you have money or not. If you follow your money, you may lose the money, and then you don't have even that.

Campbell spent four years studying literature, living a subsistence existence. While this was obviously an extreme decision, it did allow him to lay the foundation for his prolific writing about mythology, and his profound contribution to our understanding of the similarities among myths from diverse cultures worldwide.

Are you one of the lucky few who has been able to do what you love? Have there been major parts of your days and weeks where you anticipated going to work, because of getting to do what you loved? Are you in touch with what you really like doing, and ways in which to incorporate what you love into your work? Do you love creating new ways for employees to participate in the company culture? Do you love being out of doors and autonomous in your job? Do you love working with numbers and not being interrupted constantly with questions? Do you love working in an atmosphere which is open and interactive? Do you love to teach and motivate others? Do you love traveling outside the country? Do you love dressing casually rather than wearing a suit and tie every day? Do you love saving the company money by creating new, more efficient systems? Do you love having the freedom to create and implement your ideas? Do you love having to learn quickly in order to stay up with the competition? Do you love interacting with groups that are transgenerational rather than all one age? Do you love feeling secure in knowing just exactly what you are supposed to do?

If you can get back in touch with what you love, you can follow your bliss—and incorporate it into your work life. Obviously no job is all fun. The idea is to incorporate *some* of what you love in whatever jobs you are targeting, and thereby get closer to what Joseph Campbell calls "following your bliss."

8. What Were the High Points in Your Life and Work Life?

What were you doing? Where were you doing it? What characterized this as a high point for you?

Profiles: The Peaks

As mentioned in chapter 1, Edgar Mitchell discovered "nonoperational time" aboard the spacecraft to and from the moon. Beyond the excitement of being chosen to be among only twelve men who have walked on the moon, the high point for him is the deep feelings this journey elicited in him.

Staring out of the space capsule, he felt a oneness and unity with all life on the planet earth. The profoundness of this moment, this high point, led to a decision to find a way to bring spirituality and science back together so that our technology could be used for human potential rather than human destruction. Mitchell believes that early scientists made a conscious decision to steer clear of spiritual issues in order to prevent the Church from intervening in the scientific process.

In November 1987, in a speech at a two-day conference on "the Greater Self" sponsored by the Institute of Noetic Sciences in Washington, D.C., Mitchell said of the high point of his experience in space: "Seeing the same reality from a different point of view made life different." Life on earth could never be the same for him from that moment on.

It's not surprising that one of the missions of the institute he founded is to "help people change their vision of their self and their world." According to Mitchell, this is extremely important if we are to increase our ability to reach our human potential to do all we need to do at this turning point in our planet's history.

When one views the life of Robert Muller, two important experiences stand out. There were the years in which this great man was involved in education, especially in the task of working with inner-city youth who had been hardened against learning and who fell outside all the guidelines for educability that have been set in our society. Muller took on the challenge of trying to teach these students, in order to prove that everyone has learning potential if the proper channels of learning are opened. He succeeded in his experiment with these young people where all others had failed, because he had the patience to learn from them how they best liked to learn.

After serving as the Assistant Secretary-General of the United Nations, Muller became deeply involved in bringing lasting peace to the planet. As reported in the March–April 1989 edition of *New Dimensions Radio Newsletter*, he and his wife have traveled the globe, "writing, broadcasting, televising, launching ideas, inspiring, educating, corresponding, and seeing innumerable people to further the process of peace and of a better world."

Today Muller's missions of providing education to all and working toward international peace have come together in his role as Chancellor of the University for Peace in Costa Rica. The university was established in 1980 by the U.N. General Assembly as an institution devoted to educating students and promoting the possibility of full and lasting peace in our time.

What are your high points? What do you recall as being of key importance to you? What moments or experiences seemed to be absolutely key to whom you have become? Do you remember giving a particularly good talk to a professional association or writing an article that you felt was well done? Do you recall arbitrating communication between two groups of people who were unable to communicate without your help? Do you remember with particular pride making the correct decision about choice of a computer company for automation? Do you feel particularly pleased that you did not succumb to inhumane ways of dealing with unacceptable performance? What were those high points—throughout your work *and* nonwork history?

9. *What Do You Do* Like Breathing?

What do you do that comes so easily to you that you don't even have to stop and think about it—you just do it *effortlessly*, with great ease? What do you do that you yourself discount as not being important but which reflects skills that others covet because the ability does not come easily to them? What are you terrific at doing that you had no training in doing? What do you do that is "easy, effortless, and enjoyable?" to quote Michael Ray and Rochelle Myers, authors of *Creativity in Business* (Doubleday, 1986).

What you do like breathing refers to what you excel at without struggling, or perhaps without even being aware that you are excelling. It could be a talent, skill, ability that is special to you, that is integral with who you are, and on which you *may not even place a high value* because it comes so easily and is so much a part of you. Following are examples:

- An owner of a computer store that sold computers to the public for their homes or small businesses had previously had a special talent for educating. He wanted people to understand what they were buying and to feel powerful in the process rather than intimidated by computers and "computerese." He was not trying hard—the process of communicating and teaching the public just came naturally.
- A producer of a television program was an instinctive resourcer, able to come up with ideas and people and controversial subjects for discussion without even stretching her brain. It was natural to her.
- The director of a national association was skilled at interfacing with both university deans and corporate executives. He was good at translating needs from one environment to another and accomplished this portion of his job with ease.
- The director of purchasing was an instinctive "wheeler-dealer." In other words, he was instinctively good at finding a better price for product being purchased than anybody thought was possible. He loved figuring out a way to cut costs and to be creative while doing it. He was good at the strategy and negotiation—it hardly seemed like work to him.

Profile: Breathing Easy

Dee Dickinson is the founder and president of New Horizons for Learning, an international human resource network that links educators, from preschool teachers to corporate trainers. Dickinson has developed into an art form her ability to link people. She brings people together with ease, whether she is inviting a diverse group to dinner or is orchestrating an international conference on education.

Dickinson engineered a highly successful life-span learning conference that New Horizons for Learning sponsored at George Mason University in June 1988. She was thrilled that the conference gave educators from around the world the opportunity to meet, energize each other, and cross-fertilize information and insights from science and education, and from public education and the corporate classroom. The conference contributed to more effective ways to identify and meet the needs of people with different strengths, learning styles, and intelligences.

Dickinson was pleased to be able to link famous researchers from different disciplines, who might not otherwise have an opportunity to meet. No one but Dee Dickinson would think to link Dr. Marian Diamond, known for her ground-breaking work in brain research, with Dr. Howard Gardner, known for his groundbreaking work on multiple intelligences. Her ability to network appears to be a strength that she can do "like breathing" and which benefits all those interested in learning about learning.

Dickinson has a vision of a future conference in which educators around the world will be linked together by satellite. Utilizing the newest technology, it will provide people with the latest theories and practices that relate to helping people attain their intellectual capacities. This could only be the dream of a person who links people together with ease and grace.

What do you do like breathing? Do you make presentations or teach groups effortlessly? Do you link people and help cross-fertilize ideas as Dee Dickinson does? Do you listen sensitively and communicate easily? Do you write without effort, or analyze financial reports without any strain? Can you identify new strategic directions with ease? Can you differentiate effective advertising campaigns from ineffective ones because of an uncanny attention to detail? Can you motivate others to feel empowered and to do their jobs well without even trying? Do you bring energy and enthusiasm and spirit to your job—transmitting a "joie de vivre" without trying? After you identify "what you do like breathing," can you think of ways to incorporate what you uncover into your job search plan?

10. What Is Your Most Favored Intelligence, and How Do You Like to Use It?

Are you aware that you have multiple intelligences—far more than the standard two, verbal and mathematical? Are you in touch with how you best learn and in what circumstances you best acquire new information? Where are you smart?

Howard Gardner, Harvard University professor and author of *Frames of Mind: The Theory of Multiple Intelligences* (Basic Books, 1983), has developed a theory and evidence to support there being (at least) seven kinds of intelligence: 1) verbal, 2) logical/mathematical, 3) musical, 4) visual/spatial, 5) bodily/kinesthetic, 6) intrapersonal (understanding self), and 7) interpersonal (effectively interacting with others). He believes that the first two intelligences—verbal and logical/mathematical—are overvalued in our schools. Our favored intelligences often translate into favored skills and abilities. Our intellectual strengths have a decided impact on the way we think and the vantage point from which we view the world.

Profiles: Multiple Intelligences

Anyone who has watched Bill Moyers interviewing a person like Joseph Campbell, narrating a documentary, or challenging the opinions of several guests he has engaged in dialogue, can only marvel at how Moyers handles words so deftly, making the process look effortless. He exemplifies verbal intelligence at its summit.

Moyers's ability to key in on central issues, to ask simple, yet intelligent questions, is a strong factor in the popularity today of people that we might not otherwise get a chance to know, like the incomparable Joseph Campbell. Through Moyers, viewers learned about Campbell's lifelong study of myths from culture to culture. In his series titled *Man and His Myths,* Moyers was able to help the subject of myths come alive for thousands of PBS viewers by asking Joseph Campbell penetrating questions and facilitating fascinating dialogues.

Many television reporters have worked hard to rid themselves of their regional accents. Moyers is one of the few interviewers on television who retains his Texas drawl. Perhaps his drawl even contributes to his being able to bring the audience in closer. In an interview with Texas Senator Lloyd Bentsen, Moyer's comments about growing up nearby in Texas rang true as the two men spoke with similar cadences.

We met Hans Eberstark, who is from Versoix, Switzerland, at a conference sponsored by the Institute of Noetic Sciences, where he demonstrated his ability to do startling, lightning-fast mathematical calculations. Recently retired from a position as translator, he is fluent in eight languages, thereby testifying to his other well-developed intelligences and abilities as well.

In front of a large audience, Eberstark was able to multiply two five-digit numbers and arrive at the correct answer in almost less time than anyone could on their calculator. He was also able to remember and repeat fifty random numbers immediately after he heard them.

These tasks demonstrated only a minute fraction of his ability with numbers. In a hotel lobby after the lecture, Eberstark talked about his love of numbers in the same warm way that a person might describe a close friend. In fact, he had recently written an introduction to a friend's book that actually depicted numbers as characters with individual personalities. He patiently explained the meaning of excerpts from this introduction to a dozen or so people who were gathered around him that evening.

What is wonderful about Hans Eberstark is that he is a gentle, warm, friendly, nonjudgmental person who is not egotistical about his wonderful mathematical gift. He is willing to explain the methodology of how he does his calculations to anyone who has the interest to listen.

Attending one of Don Campbell's music workshops is an introduction to his deep belief in the importance of music and sound. Each participant is encouraged to move his body, close his eyes, and get in touch with his own musical rhythms. ("Hear that sound? Think that it is the sound of waves hitting the shore? Well, no. That is the sound of the mother's inhalations and exhalations as heard from the perspective of the child in womb." No wonder we so often seek relaxation near the seashore!)

Don Campbell has the wonderful ability to convince anyone who attends his workshops of the magic and marvel of music and sound. For more than twenty years Campbell has been teaching music in classrooms from elementary through secondary school. Today as director of the Institute for Music, Health, and Education, located in Texas and Colorado, he remains committed to spreading the message about the importance of integrating music into the curriculum—not just to round out the student, but in order to develop musical intelligence.

At the Conference on Life-Span Learning, in June 1988, Campbell said: "Intelligence and knowledge are modified by the ways in which these sonic and rhythmic patterns are impressed upon the mind of the developing child." For too long music has been taught only for the purpose of developing performance skills and for personal enrichment. Campbell believes that the time has come to use music to enhance the learning capacities of all students.

At thirty-two, Buckminster Fuller seriously considered committing suicide, so bleak was life for him at a time when he felt he couldn't support his family. But something gave him the courage to go on. At that point, according to Richard Brenneman, editor of *Fuller's Earth: A Day with Bucky and the Kids* (St. Martin's Press, 1984), "Bucky" instead resolved to turn his knowledge of technology toward a new aim—what he called *livingry*, the solving of humanity's life problems.

One of the challenges he addressed was architectural—to create buildings called geodesic domes that enclosed more space with less material than any structure previously devised by man. Today geodesic domes span the globe or "Spaceship Earth," as Bucky liked to call our planet. A good example of this structure, which looks like a giant igloo made out of a series of equilateral triangular panes of glass, can be seen at the St. Louis Botanical Gardens.

Aside from being an architect, poet, cosmic chronicler, and philosopher, Buckminster Fuller was also an inventor. He created many things that were designed to solve human problems. Among them was a shower that allows the user to bathe with a fine mist from just one pint of water. This invention is a good example of Bucky's principle of ephemeralization—finding ways to do more with less. Ultimately, he wanted to maximize our efficiencies so that we could feed all of humanity. He believed that there are enough resources to go around and to make the world work—if the resources are used efficiently and effectively.

Anybody who watched Greg Louganis dive in the Olympic competition would agree that his bodily/kinesthetic intelligence was in top form. As a youngster, Louganis demonstrated intelligence in this arena and eventually moved in with his coach to concentrate on developing his abilities to their pinnacle. The grace and control that he demonstrated quite literally took one's breath away—so hard was it to believe that one person could have such an incredible degree of power and control over his body.

Thinking back to our experiences in the bodily/kinesthetic areas, most of us received societal and cultural messages that we were *either* smart *or* well coordinated. Athletes with good minds were anomalies—deviations from the norm. Intellects were labeled "eggheads" and often stuck to their books rather than testing their intelligence in athletics. Gym teachers were former "jocks" and low in status. Physics teachers were scholars and high in status. Students with interests in the bodily/kinesthenic arena might have repressed those interests in order to follow career tracks that were more socially acceptable.

Well, times have changed. Fitness centers and wellness experts have hit the corporate arena at full speed, and corporations now realize that the mind and body are intimately related—that exercise of the body will have a dramatic impact on the quality of the mind's output.

Do you have bodily/kinesthetic intelligence? Are you interested in finding ways to build that intelligence into your next work endeavor?

Intrapersonal intelligence is a highly developed and keen understanding of one's self. Actors must have intrapersonal intelligence in order to go deeply within themselves to find the elements that compose the character they are portraying on stage or screen. No actor celebrates this ability more than John Mahoney, who spent thirty-seven years of his life living up to the expectations of others.

John Mahoney is now one of Hollywood's busiest actors. He played Richard Dreyfus's partner in *Tin Men,* the murderous judge in *Suspect,* the dinner companion who failed to charm Olympia Dukakis in *Moonstruck,* and recently starred in *Say Anything.* Yet a little more than ten years ago, Mahoney was working in Chicago as an editor, a culmination of a number of jobs he had pursued instead of acting. Like many in our society, he was dissuaded from acting, fearing lack of security and stability. But after seeing a stage production in London, he experienced a renewed determination to follow his earlier dream and become an actor. He soon began acting lessons and joined a theater company in Chicago.

Mahoney was discovered and offered film parts when he appeared on stage in New York in *Orphans.* Even though it took tremendous courage to completely turn his life around, John Mahoney believes that it was all worth it. He says that his friends think he is much nicer now—less critical and impatient with others. He believes this is because he is now less critical and impatient with himself.

Anyone who has watched Phil Donahue perform as host of his daily national talk show must admire his ability to interact with guests and audiences. He has an uncanny ability to cajole people into disclosing personal, private information immediately after he has suggested that the person is free to withhold it. Different from other talk show hosts, Donahue treats each guest with complete respect. His questions may be difficult and probing, but he separates the issue from the person, careful to protect the dignity of whomever he is engaging in conversation.

A good example of his consummate interpersonal ability has been displayed during the space-bridge television shows that he has conducted with American and Soviet citizens, both in the United States and in the Soviet Union. As an ambassador of good will, Donahue facilitated interaction among his international audiences, chipping away at and helping to dissipate distrusts and misconceptions that have existed for many years. In the programs that he shared with the Soviet personality Vladimir Posner, Donahue displayed a warmth and a willingness to share the stage with a colleague from an Eastern country.

Nowhere is Donahue's interpersonal intelligence more evident than backstage after a taping of his show. He can be seen standing patiently while hundreds of people stand in line waiting to shake his hand, ask for his autograph, and chat about the show.

Do these case studies of different kinds of intelligence trigger any thoughts about yourself? Can you identify which kinds of intelligence are your preferences? Which ones are better developed than others? Have there been ample opportunities for you to exercise and "grow" your intelligences in your previous positions? Have you had the opportunity to develop your intelligences by stretching to meet new demands of your jobs?

Companies will be competing for human resources in the 1990s, due to the decreasing work force population, and they will be looking for ways to stimulate and engage future employees as learners as well as contributors to the bottom line. Throughout *Re-inventing the Corporation*, John Naisbitt and Patricia Aburdene cite examples of innovative companies that have begun to focus in on how to attract and retain good employees. The authors even give examples of forward-thinking companies that offer sabbaticals to employees after a certain number of years—aware that the focus on learning and personal growth is rapidly becoming a priority to employees.

Is it a priority for you? Do you want to stretch outside the boundaries that you have either consciously or unconsciously set for yourself or the parameters set forth by your previous job descriptions?

Identifying Options for Employment—
Generating Multiple Job Scenarios

Throughout this chapter you have been thinking back over your career, remembering what skills and abilities you like to use, weaknesses that could be turned into strengths, avocational interests, and career fantasies. You have taken the time to focus in on your visions, any sense of mission you currently have, passions, and high points. You are probably clear about the areas in which you are qualified. You have taken the time to identify specific goals which may relate to your mission or your areas of effectiveness. In addition, you may have identified areas of interest that you plan to explore further.

Now is a good time to go back through your notes and thoughts up to this point and isolate possible directions, or job scenarios, that you would like to explore. One direction will undoubtedly be similar to the job you have just left, either in your industry or other industries that interest you.

At this point in your job search, you may also want to identify a number of different options, some related directly to your previous positions, and others perhaps not so directly related. Having multiple job scenarios to explore can give you greater flexibility in choosing a direction that will be right for you. It can help prevent you from narrowing your vision at the expense of your opportunities. It can keep you energized and stimulated.

A problem that many job searchers have is that they do not think expansively enough about directions worth pursuing. Generating multiple job scenarios to explore will contribute to your freedom of choice and will prevent you from counting on any single target that may not ultimately work out.

For example, a former senior vice president of a major hospital did a careful analysis of his unique dimensions and generated the following specific scenarios to explore:

1. Replication of similar position in a major hospital.
2. President of a smaller hospital.
3. Director of strategic planning/marketing for any health-care institution—including HMOs or PPOs—that need planning.
4. Senior account manager at an advertising agency.
5. Executive in a health-care association.
6. Director of strategic planning in industry, outside of health care.
7. Assistant to the president of any smaller business, responsible for marketing, planning, or operations.
8. Retainer headhunter for a local agency, as an entrepreneur, or for a national company planning to open a new agency in his hometown.
9. Consultant for a big-eight CPA firm specializing in health care or strategic planning/marketing.

As you pull together a number of different directions, you will be identifying the threads of your job search and expanding your possibilities. You may place a different emphasis on one scenario over another, but you can always return to your list to evaluate whether your search should be redefined.

In order to carefully catalogue the options that have emerged from your search into yourself throughout this chapter, you may want to start a notebook in which you devote a separate page or pages to each direction you intend to explore. For each scenario, jot down names of people or organizations worth contacting in this field. As you continue to network throughout your search, you can begin to expand the contacts for each scenario you are exploring. If you keep careful records of whom you spoke with in regard to each scenario, perhaps exploring one scenario one week and another the next, you will avoid becoming confused during your search.

In this way, even though you will be pursuing multiple options, you will not feel as if you are all over the map. Now is the time for you to access your organizational skills—the ones that helped you achieve as much as you have this far in your career. Create some systems that will serve you well throughout your job search.

Environments/Cultures/ Life Cycles

You have now completed analyzing your unique dimensions and generated a list of scenarios to explore. Before you actually begin your job search in earnest, you can apply your analytical skills to evaluating potential organizational environments and cultures and think through what characteristics most appeal to you. Additionally, you can do some thinking about what stage in its organizational life cycle a company should be for you to be most attracted to working there. We'll define what we mean by "organizational life cycle" a little later on.

Have you given much thought to what kind of environment appeals to you the most or what kind of company culture best contributes to your operating at your best? Do you have a fast pace, wanting to get things done in a hurry and carrying a number of balls simultaneously, or do you prefer to operate in a slower, more deliberate way, giving yourself time to carefully think through the repercussions of your actions and decisions?

Much has been written about corporate cultures in recent years and the impact of the culture on the employees within it. Any dissonance between your preferred environment or culture and that within which you work can actually be a contributing factor to being terminated. We recall one former client who had been with his company as an industrial engineer for a number of years when the management changed. Before too long, he was fired from his position, not because he was ineffective, but primarily because his

pace was perceived as too slow by the new team. It didn't matter that his careful attention to detail had prevented mishaps and had actually saved the company time and money. The manager to whom he now reported just saw him as being too slow. He was eventually able to find a position in a company that didn't place such an inordinate value on speed of activity and performance. They appreciated his thoughtful, deliberate pace.

Another client, who had outstanding accounting expertise, was fired partly because he "couldn't keep his nose out of everyone else's business." Up until meeting with us, he assumed that he *had* erred in a major way and that his way of operating was inappropriate. It was just that he really wanted to understand how the company worked and feel more connected with the other functional areas within his company than he had for the previous four years. He decided to target accounting positions within companies that viewed employees as dynamic and which encouraged what Tom Peters, bestselling author of *In Search of Excellence,* calls "managing by wandering around (MBWA)." In his new job there was a strong ethic *not* to remain separate, but instead to promote interaction and cross-fertilization with all other departments.

Much has been written about Gore Industries, founded by Bill Gore, who invented Gore-Tex—the material that breathes while remaining entirely waterproof. Gore created a culture with a flat organization chart, in which all employees are called "associates" and are given considerable power and control over their work lives. In fact, it is well known that at Gore Industries it is not at all uncommon for a newly recruited employee to be told to "find something to do" that would contribute to the company in the best way he or she can discover. One story that hit the grapevine involves a Gore employee who wanted a title and a business card reflecting that title. When she spoke to Bill Gore about her desires, he told her to choose her own title—and she eventually chose "supreme commander" to be on *her* business card.

Are you attracted to working in a company with the reflected values and ethic of Gore Industries? Or do you prefer to work where there are clearly delineated job descriptions and career tracks? What's important here is for you to think through honestly what appeals most to you—in what culture you would be most productive.

Tom Peters tells a story on one of his recent videos that a colleague related to him. It concerned a certain service station that had the strongest value on customer service his colleague had ever experienced. When she drove into the service station and up to the pumps, she was met by several employees who simultaneously cleaned the inside and outside of her car, filled up the tank and checked the oil, and provided her with coffee, doughnut, and newspaper. And all of this with good humor, friendly conversation, and obvious respect for the customer. After hearing the story, Peters said that he was inclined to visit the service station just for the experience of it—even if he didn't need fuel!

Do you want to align yourself with a company that is conscious about the importance of the customer? Do you want contact with customers, or do you prefer to work away from the customer base?

Peters gives the viewer a close look at the culture of a variety of very successful companies who are experimenting with alternative cultures in his video. One company includes employees in policy-making meetings and reflects a belief in the importance of personal growth, learning, and cross-training by systematically rewarding these areas with salary increases. The energy and commitment of these employees were almost palpable.

Do you want to work in a company with a climate like this? Or do you prefer one where traditional lines of authority are drawn? The trick in evaluating your own preferences lies in not judging either as better than the other. Where would you feel most comfortable, and where would you be most productive and happiest in the long term?

Many companies are experimenting with physical space, and

creating open areas rather than large private offices. Some of these same companies are testing the success of greater emphasis on teams or partnerships, especially across functional areas. Feedback sessions in some companies are standard—feedback from employees to managers to evaluate what is and is not working.

Some of these companies have employees training their managers in the use of the computer and the analysis of data—areas which had passed the managers by because their formal education just missed the new technology and they had been used to delegating these activities to others. Other companies are experimenting with groups and teams doing their own hiring and firing, and conducting their own performance appraisals. Are you attracted to cultures like these, or do you prefer more traditional, built-in training programs and performance appraisals directly from your manager?

Some companies are actually experimenting with giving sabbaticals to long-time employees. Sometimes the sabbatical can be requested after as few as four years of employment. These companies are aware that several weeks or even months off to retrain or reinvest in new experiences or learning endeavors can pay off when the employee returns to the job. Are any of these variables important to you? Could you build them into a job offer if they are? Can you think of ways to uncover the company culture during your interview process?

And what about the actual physical surroundings in which you will work? Do you feel more attracted to newer or older buildings? Is light important to you? Does it matter whether it is an urban or a rural setting? What about the windows—do they open, or is it a high-rise without that option? Do you want/need the freedom to decorate your own space? Does it matter whether there are private conference-room facilities? How about the background music—is it Muzak, and does that bother you at all? You don't need to feel embarrassed to realize that one kind of physical setting is important to you. Many job searchers neglect to consider the physical setting and then find themselves unhappy after the fact because they didn't take these variables into consideration.

Organizational Life Cycles

One can hardly pick up a *Wall Street Journal* today without seeing a story about a merger or an acquisition or a downsizing or a start-up. It is not at all uncommon to read about an imminent business failure or a company that just went into chapter 11. It is commonplace for a privately held organization to go public or a venture capital firm to close down a company not meeting its quarterly earnings projections. Foreign investors abound, and the global economy is obviously a different economy than the one we studied in school and for which we were educated.

Unfortunately we have not had the benefit of classes in change management. We have not been prepared for how to keep our careers on an even keel in the midst of industry upheaval, threat of buyouts, or foreign investors. We are just beginning to be aware of the truth of the adage "The only constant is change."

But the impact of all of these changes on our jobs and careers is enormous. You are possibly experiencing the effect of one of these changes—it may have contributed to your being without a job. And what *is* the effect of all of these changes? Well, for one thing, the size and structure and culture of the company in which you find yourself could change almost instantaneously, and you might feel as if you are in an altogether different company with the same name. We have heard from senior executives in major corporations that a new boss can even make a manager feel as if he is in an entirely new job—even if nothing else had changed.

Bob noticed, when thinking through the periods of time in which he was happiest, that his time of greatest satisfaction in his work was when he was working for a relatively young organization that tended to go out of its way to recognize the individual efforts of its employees. It was not at all uncommon for the president to comment on the outstanding work he was doing in establishing manufacturing facilities, particularly complimenting him on his safety programs. When this privately held company sold out to a public company, everything changed. Many senior managers were replaced—and the new owners brought in their own teams. Budgets were scrutinized and slashed. The employee retreat center was sold. But most significant to Bob was the decreased support of creative thinking—having a direct impact on his freedom to experiment with the facilities he was designing and building. And it had been months since anyone had noticed or complimented him on anything he had done.

Bob was keenly aware of his attraction to a more familial environment, where he felt important and visible and where he could experiment in order to make things better. He decided to target privately held companies and tried to identify industries that he believed were less likely to be vulnerable to merger mania, though of course he couldn't know for certain.

So where in the cycle of an organization are you most comfortable? A small, entrepreneurial start-up or a large, more layered organization? A company which values "intrapreneurship" like the 3M company, or an organization with more clearly defined job descriptions and a lower value on experimentation? A company which has all kinds of opportunities for you to develop your career because of its size, or a smaller company which might dead-end for you unless you can invent new ways to bring value to the company? A company in a volatile industry or one that has not yet succumbed to merger mania?

Large or small? Personal or not? Start-up or mature? Private or public? As you contemplate your alternatives and target the scenarios that you have decided to pursue, we urge you to be true to yourself and honest about what would make you happiest.

4

3-D Marketing

Your Opportunity to Communicate
Your Uniqueness

Ron Toran was working at a Massachusetts financial services company as a marketing representative to banks when he saw an advertisement in the *American Banker,* a daily trade publication in the banking industry, for a sales position selling software programs to major banks. According to the ad, the candidate needed five to six years in banking and sales experience to qualify for consideration. The salary plus commission offered would more than double his present salary.

Knowing that his year and a half of experience as a marketing rep in the financial services industry and his work experience throughout his innovative work-study college program might not be taken seriously, Ron looked for a way to communicate his uniqueness and become three-dimensional. He really wanted an interview and a chance to sell himself in person.

So along with his chronological résumé he sent a five-minute videotape that he created himself on a newly purchased cam corder. On the video, Ron introduced himself and explained that his credentials were actually a lot stronger than reflected on his résumé. He described what he was doing in his present job, and related his qualifications directly to those stated in the advertisement. He also mentioned the names of several references and how they could be contacted.

When Ron followed up his mailing with a phone call, the secretary told him that the individual to whom he had written was on the road and had not yet been through his mail. Shortly thereafter, Ron received a call from the hiring manager, who told him that they had been very impressed with Ron's creative approach to presenting himself. They liked his creativity because they considered themselves to be a creative company. But they could not consider him for the position he had responded to since they believed that selling large data-processing systems to multibillion-dollar banks would be way over his head.

Ron continued to present his case, however, knowing that this call could lead to alternate possibilities. He was told that he would be contacted by another person who was expanding a different division of the company involved with sales of systems to banks in smaller communities. When Ron was contacted not long afterward, he was acutely aware that his telephone skills were being evaluated as they spoke. The caller wanted to discuss the range of experience Ron had in contacting senior-level bank executives.

Because he handled himself so well on the telephone, he was invited to Florida at the company's expense for a series of interviews for a job which he had not originally known existed. During the course of the interviews, he learned that several others, who had five to ten years' more direct experience than he had, were also being considered. Yet in the final analysis Ron was offered the job due to his style and approach and found himself in a position that had unlimited earning potential. In fact, Ron's first commission check was double his previous year's salary.

Ron had a clear sense of his own personal drive and unique style and approach and searched until he found a way to communicate these to potential employers. He demonstrated who he was, what he had done in the past, and what he was capable of doing in the future through his video and résumé.

Our challenge is to help you develop the techniques that will help *you* market yourself as well as Ron did—not necessarily through videotapes, but definitely through effective use of the written word. We'll assist you in becoming *three-dimensional* through use of résumés, letters, proposals, and portfolios, so that you can stand out above the crowd of mediocre or average marketing communications.

You are undoubtedly aware of the need for a résumé if you have been scanning the papers and have seen the inevitable words "Send résumé." Or perhaps former colleagues have told you, "Send me your résumé, and I'll forward it on to Joe, who I know has been looking for a person like you." But have you thought about writing a résumé that will be useful for the number of diverse job scenarios you'll be exploring? Or writing several résumés?

Chances are you have never thought of how a proposal could project you forward into the job that you may be interviewing for next week. Unlike a graphic artist, architect, or public relations executive, you may not have thought of the possibility of using a portfolio of your past work to help fill in the blanks about your capabilities and skills.

Even if you have written numerous business proposals in your previous job(s), you probably haven't thought about how a proposal presented either during or after an interview might propel you into the position, either. And while you might have thought about the fact that a good cover letter would need to accompany your résumé through the mail, you might not have considered the other uses for letters that we will explore later in this chapter.

So what we hope to accomplish in this chapter is to help you become aware of the many options you have to present yourself on paper.

To stimulate your appreciation for the positive results that can occur from some effort with the written word during the job-search campaign, here is a preview of what happened to some of our clients:

- A client sent a résumé in answer to an ad in a professional journal and was invited in for an interview—one of only several other candidates out of hundreds who had applied—because of the clarity and professionalism of his résumé.
- A woman sent a well-crafted letter to the head of a department in a company she was targeting. On the basis of this letter, she was offered a free-lance assignment and eventually a position within the company.
- A job searcher reluctantly traveled to Pittsburgh for an interview (she never thought she'd like Pittsburgh) and was offered a job because of the impression her portfolio made on the hiring committee—in a field where no one else uses portfolios.

The First Dimension—Résumés
That Capture Your Uniqueness

The very *thought* of writing a résumé may make you cringe, may trigger feelings of extreme distaste. Writing a résumé may feel to you about as attractive a task as volunteering to collect money for an unpopular political candidate. You might have to suppress the initial urge to call a résumé-writing service. After all, you don't want to put the fate of your entire job search in the hands of someone who hardly even knows you and cannot possibly imagine the depth of your talent and skill. Resist the urge, hang in with us, and we'll help you successfully translate yourself to résumé format. The final result will reflect your own unique vocabulary, perspective, energy, and character.

The problem with developing a résumé is that no matter how brilliant and articulate it may be, it is *still* just pieces of paper full of a lot of words. And it still just reflects where you have been (your past) rather than projecting you into the future of the company you are targeting. A résumé can never be remotely as effective as the three-dimensional you could be in personally promoting yourself.

However, if you directly participate in creating your own résumé, you will have an infinitely better chance of reflecting your special blend of experience and skills and strengths than if you go to a résumé-writing service. Your résumé will use vocabulary in a way that you typically express yourself and in jargon appropriate for your industry or special area of expertise. It will sound like you talking. It will be congruent with your personal presentation style. No one will look at your résumé and wonder why you hired a service rather than taking the time and energy to develop your own.

The résumé is the ultimate marketing tool. It is a key method of self-promotion. It is a personal advertisement. It is a careful presentation of the data about yourself that focuses the reader while it tells your story.

An effective résumé does not require the reader to work hard to figure out what you have that might be valuable to her. She doesn't have to make the translation between your past and her future. You've done the translation for her. One of the most valuable results of developing a résumé is how positive it makes you feel about yourself.

The bottom line is this: You want someone to scan or read your résumé and want to meet you. Or if they have met you, you want your résumé to accurately reflect the interaction they had when they met you. You want such a strong résumé that even if your résumé is received in the final stages of a search, it stimulates re-opening the search. That is exactly what happened with a client (an attorney) looking for a corporate legal position. The financial services institution that was creating an in-house legal-counsel position had narrowed down the selection to the final three—and had even finished the first round of interviews with these three candidates. Our client's résumé surfaced through a contact who hand-delivered it, and the search was reopened to include him for consideration.

Come Meet Our Friends

We asked ourselves how we could write a chapter on résumés, letters, proposals, and portfolios that would be interesting to you. How could we make it warm and friendly? How could we use it as a positive stimulus for your writing to begin? Then it occurred to us—we'd do something different from other job-search books. We'd introduce you to many of our clients/friends, share with you their thinking and hopes and dreams, and then show you the résumé they developed to market themselves. In this way you'd see how the résumé evolved naturally out of the person's purpose and potential audience.

Meet Adam, an individual in his forties with a twinkle in his eye, a compliment for everyone, and a highly expert technical background. He had been employed for nearly twenty years in manufacturing management in the chemical industry, working for a company when it was small, privately held, and like a family. He participated in its growth and expansion, took pride in the reinforcement and recognition he received for his fine contributions.

As Adam explored possibilities for himself, he generated a number of different scenarios. One was a duplication of his past position, a senior position in manufacturing management. Another was involved with safety, an area in which he had become extremely knowledgeable. A third was with some area of corporate fitness and wellness, emphasizing its relationship to safety as well as its preventive role in physical and mental health.

A traditional, chronological résumé would not have given Adam the flexibility that he needed to explore these diverse possibilities. He wanted a format which would present him as accomplished and would prevent others from viewing him as "manufacturing manager" or as simply "qualified for the chemical industry." So he opted for developing a résumé headed not by a specific job objective but by a personal summary that would work for each of the options he was considering. (See exhibit A.)

His personal summary was designed to highlight the method in which he conducted his work and whet the appetite of the reader for more. The next decision Adam made was to write his résumé functionally rather than chronologically, to choose areas of effectiveness that summarized the expertise and aspects of his background that he wanted to emphasize. He asked himself the following questions: What do I know? What are my main areas of expertise? What am I good at doing? How can I look at all my experience and organize it not in terms of job titles, but in terms of patterns of demonstrated expertise?

While Adam was considering what areas of effectiveness to include, he had to remind himself of the scenarios he was going to explore. He wanted the résumé to speak to each of the scenarios he was seriously considering. He wanted it to trigger relevant questions in interviews. Adam chose the following areas of effectiveness: Operations/Facilities Management, Engineering/Facilities Construction, and Quality Assurance/Safety.

Under each of his areas of effectiveness, Adam listed specific examples from throughout his work experience. He was not restricted to a chronological order but could really present patterns of accomplishments effectively.

As Adam developed his résumé, he continually asked himself the question, "Would this résumé work for each of the scenarios that I have decided to explore? Does it reflect what I know? Does it sound like me talking?"

The conclusion of his résumé—after a listing of his jobs and

Exhibit A
ADAM SANDERS
Address
Phone

Personal Summary

A Senior Executive with solid background in operations management in a manufacturing environment who exhibits exceptional skills in people development, process flow, scheduling, engineering, construction, and safety in the workplace.

PROFESSIONAL EXPERIENCE

Operations Facilities Management

Responsible for manufacturing operations of three production facilities in the U.S. and a toll (contract) manufacturer in Canada. Corporate support functions encompassed customer service, purchasing, manufacturing services, and warehouse and distribution. Duties included establishment of operating budgets, coordination of production flow, and maintenance of adequate inventory levels, with a total staff of 220 people.

- Directed the manufacturing of an extensive, complex product line from three facilities within established budget guidelines of $7.5 million to meet sales demands of $90 million.

- Increased plant capacity of the largest of three production facilities by 250% through complete reorganization of production flow and implementation of detailed scheduling procedures with no increase in headcount.

- Increased the service level for on-time delivery from an average of 70% to a high of 95% to meet guidelines set by sales and marketing.

- *This résumé, and others, in this section actually take up only two to three pages when word processed or printed on letter sized paper.*

ADAM SANDERS
Phone
Page Two

- Conducted the successful negotiations of labor contracts with two separate labor unions, holding settlements within guidelines established by top management.

- Managed the conversion of purchased facility during a demand period, resulting in no loss of momentum.

- Provided manufacturing input for the design of a computerized data processing system and implemented cycle count procedures at plant levels, resulting in a high degree of inventory integrity leading to reduced downtime for physical inventory.

- Managed the corporate purchasing function that provided approximately $400 M bottom-line profit as a result of initiating negotiated purchase contracts, duty drawbacks, and prudent purchase controls.

- Directed the management of the company's warehouse and distribution system, consisting of some 22 strategic locations throughout the world. Reduced overall inventory dollars in warehouse while increasing service level.

- Developed a strong, service-oriented customer-service organization sensitive to customer needs, with increased respect for production schedules and demands.

- Organized company-owned trucking system for delivery of specialty division's products and effectively reduced delivery costs to zero with the back haul of a variety of raw materials.

- Traveled extensively overseas providing manufacturing support to foreign affiliates and negotiated with independent firms for the production of product line in Canada, resulting in a lower cost to Canadian sales and increased volume.

ADAM SANDERS
Phone
Page Three

Engineering/Facilities Construction

- Designed and supervised the construction of several large production and warehouse expansions from 13,000 sq. ft. to 96,000 sq. ft. and coordinated the company's capital expenditure program of projects, totaling over $1.5 million.

- Evaluated at pilot-plant level numerous pieces of innovative production equipment, resulting in process installations providing improved quality and product consistency as well as increased efficiency.

- Initiated the project and collaborated in the design of a highly automated production line that resulted in a 50% manpower reduction.

- To prevent the closing of a facility, and after obtaining expensive bid quotations, designed and installed waste-water treatment facility. Upon completion, gained one of a limited number of EPA permits for discharge into a national scenic waterway.

- Consolidated major warehouse operation into one large building having specially designed bin system for effective order picking, resulting in 30% manpower reduction.

Quality Assurance/Safety

- Implemented company's first quality-assurance program at plant level to comply with Nuclear Regulatory Standards, with the eventual certification of all three facilities.

- Expanded in-process checks and enhanced operator training in procedures and techniques, which resulted in a substandard-product generation of less than 1% of volume produced.

- Developed the original concept of a program of Quality Circles and formed the first employee circle. Program has grown to include all plant and office locations, necessitating a full-time corporate facilitator.

ADAM SANDERS
Phone
Page Four

- Represented corporation as an internal consultant for the study, design, and implementation of a safety and plant-protection program involving 10 locations, resulting in major reduction in loss-time injuries and overall reduction in insurance rates.

- Taking a proactive approach, conducted audits of facilities to ensure OSHA compliance prior to actual inspections, which then resulted in minimal exposure.

- Organized plant safety programs to promote safety awareness among employees, resulting in major reduction of accidents and lost time.

Work Experience

————   1970–present

Director of Manufacturing Operations—Western Region
Manager of Manufacturing—St. Louis, Missouri
Plant Manager—Xenia, Ohio

————   1959–1970

Production Manager—Trades Sales Plant—Houston, Texas
Project Engineer—Corporate
Project Engineer—Louisville Plant
New Product Liaison with Manufacturing
Formulator Product Development Group

————   1957–1958

Debit Salesman; Management Trainee

Education and Training

University of Dayton and Wright State University   1970–1974
  Business/Management Courses

ADAM SANDERS
Phone
Page Five

University of Louisville	1958–1959

Chemical Engineering

The Citadel Military College	1953–1956

Predental/Chemistry

Numerous in-house training including the following: 1970–1983

- Kepner-Tregoe—"Apex II Problem Solving"
- IBM—"Data Processing for Managers"
- American Management Association—"MRP Materials Requirement Planning"
- National Paint & Coating Association—"Small Plant Design"
- Hazardous Waste Association—"Handling of Hazardous Waste"
- National Fire Protection Association—
  "Flammable Liquids and Static Electricity"
- OSHA Region V—"OSHA in the Workplace"

Special Interests

- Keeping physically fit by working out: running, competitive racquetball, and playing golf are routine, relaxing, and permit me to gain the maximum from mind and body to perform efficiently and effectively.

- Served as the initial contact for a pioneer employee-assistance program designed to provide support in personal-needs areas such as finance, child care, alcoholism, and drug abuse.

employing organizations—included two categories, Education and Training, and Special Interests. He felt it crucial that he describe his interest in staying physically fit, as well as his involvement in developing the company employee-assistance program from its inception. Neither of these was superfluous information; each directly related to a couple of the scenarios he was considering.

Adam had given up smoking and initiated a serious exercise program in his life a few years earlier. He deeply believed that his life-style change not only enhanced his performance but increased his energy, productivity, and leadership abilities. Having them listed as strong interests could only enhance the picture of him, could only build a stronger case for the appropriateness of his current job focus.

Adam conducted a fascinating job search, uncovering possibilities for himself even further afield than he originally anticipated. He rarely used a résumé, especially if he initiated the meeting and the résumé was not requested. The résumé did, however, become committed to memory, with the specific accomplishments and special areas of interest indelibly imprinted on his memory. And often, if he hadn't left a résumé behind, he would send one with a follow-up letter or send a longer form letter he had developed which incorporated information from the résumé.

Meet Pamela, most recently a real estate analyst for a major corporation, with her position reporting through the treasury department. Pamela had a strong presence, a ready smile, and a deep sense of integrity that jumped out at you upon first meeting her. She was particularly open to considering options in settings other than corporate real estate functions, where she had been working for several years.

When developing scenarios to explore, Pamela thought a great deal about her own personal experience in real estate. She was aware of an unmet need in the industry—more formalized advanced training for individuals in her field—which was necessary to advance the stature of working in the industry. She herself would have appreciated having had the opportunity to attend a program similar to the one she was thinking about designing and implementing at a college in her community. Pamela explored this idea with gusto until she realized that the academic realm is as structured as the corporate world. She also was worried about acceptance, since she did not have a college degree. Finally, it became clear that if she was able to pull it off, it certainly would not be within the time frame necessary for her to be reemployed.

Pamela was also committed to the idea of assisting others in building solid investment portfolios to assure their financial future. Combining her own passion for assisting others in making wise investments with her knowledge and interest in real estate led to her actual career decision. She started her own business, putting together real estate investment packages for the ordinary consumer. Her ultimate goal was to assist individuals in good long-term financial planning.

Pamela did a fairly nontraditional job search, pursuing almost totally her own ideas rather than responding to already existing job openings. She did not investigate replicating her position as real estate analyst responsible for corporate real estate purchase, sale, and leasing decisions. (She decided not to reenter the corporate world.) She rarely used a résumé since she was usually armed with a written proposal of some sort. But she did develop a résumé, just in case she wanted to respond to a possibility that required one. (See exhibit B.)

For her traditional, chronological résumé, Pamela chose to use both an objective and a professional summary. She believed that including both would build a wider picture of her capabilities. Her objective was written broadly enough to reflect her talents without restricting her options.

Her professional summary demonstrated the depth of her experience in terms of years and expertise and was designed to combat the resistance she might get from potential employers who, seeing that she had not completed a college education, might not take her seriously. The chronological format Pamela chose emphasized her corporate experience, with her specific accomplishments during these eight years listed in order of their importance and quantified wherever possible. Her experience with a title insurance company, as a senior escrow officer, and with a real estate company, as an associate broker specializing in land sales to developers, were listed in descending chronological order after her corporate experience. She concluded the résumé with a listing of her eight-year involvement in her family's real estate firm.

Since Pamela's formal education included only two years of college, she listed specific classes and seminars, as well as dis-

Exhibit B
PAMELA STOKES
Address
Phone

___

Objective

Position utilizing my vast experience in real estate acquisitions and asset management with an emphasis on financial results, where my commitment to the evolution of the professional stature of the real estate industry will be supported and encouraged.

Professional Summary

As a result of family ties with both a title and development company, my experience with real estate began in adolescence. Since then, career progressions ranging from title and escrow officer through broker to analyst in an international Fortune 100 corporation with real estate assets of over $1 billion have provided an in-depth exposure to the multidisciplinary aspects of the real estate industry.

Professional Experience

————, Corporate Real Estate Department 1976–present
St. Louis, Missouri

Real Estate Analyst, reporting through Treasury Department

Real estate advice and counsel to the Manager, Domestic Financial Analysis/Real Estate. Responsible for purchase, sale, and lease of corporate real estate; management of underutilized property for income; creating department policy; hiring agents, appraisers, and consultants; and developing creative alternatives for purchase and sale of various types of corporate facilities, with an emphasis on after-tax results.

- Located and negotiated purchase or lease of all St. Louis facilities, including land, office buildings, research facilities, and warehouses.

- Located and negotiated purchase of Chesterfield Village, 210-acre site for adjunct research headquarters of ————, the largest

PAMELA STOKES
Phone
Page Two

project currently under construction in St. Louis—$175 MM. Approximate current market value of the land is 200% of 1979 cost.

- Recommended conversion of warehouse space to interim research facilities, resulting in cost reduction of 50% of new construction costs and acceleration of program start-up.

- Identified excess office space, Atlanta sales office. Recommended and implemented sublease program resulting in additional income to —— of $200 M over lease term and estimated $330 M during the extended term, thus offsetting 42% of entire —— rent expense.

- Initiated agricultural lease review program and recommended farm management program resulting in 800% increase in income.

- Negotiated leases for all major offices nationwide with resulting 10% to 20% overall improvement in terms.

- Developed strategy using various tax incentives to enable replacement of an antiquated Connecticut facility with a modern, energy-efficient plant at no capital cost to the corporation, resulting in significant operating cost reductions.

- In 1982, handled projects involving $18.9 MM, with resulting savings to the corporation of $2.6 MM.

——   1973–1976

St. Louis, Missouri

Senior Escrow Officer

Responsible for closing all types of real estate transactions, including investment properties and mortgages. Authored escrow agreements related to construction completion, investment of funds, and resolution of legal matters.

PAMELA STOKES
Phone
Page Three

- As escrow officer effected almost 100%, on-time closings through preparation, counseling, advice, and negotiation with agents, principals, and attorneys to resolve unforeseen problems.

- Exclusive closing officer to major commercial and industrial firms, consummating monthly, multimillion-dollar transactions.

- Trained and supervised escrow trainees and clericals.

—————   1972–1973

St. Louis, Missouri

Associated Broker, Advertising Manager

- Specialized in land sales to developers. Obtained bids for soil engineering tests, utility installations, zoning, and other data to provide a complete cost picture to prospective developers.

- Produced intensive sales training programs for 30 agents on the legal implications of contract clauses as well as closing procedures and land measurements to upgrade professionalism and service to clientele.

—————   1969–1972

St. Louis, Missouri

Escrow Officer
Title Officer

—————   1961–1969

St. Louis, Missouri

Vice President

Responsible for office administration and advertising for family-owned real estate business.

PAMELA STOKES
Phone
Page Four

Education and Continued Professional Growth

Washington University, St. Louis, Missouri, 2 years

Additional Classes and Seminars in:

Office leasing, communications, asset management, negotiating skills, and others.

Distinctions

- Missouri Real Estate Broker
- 1st Woman Title Examiner in ————
- Current YWCA Outstanding Woman Leader Nominee

Professional and Community Associations

- National Association of Corporate Real Estate Executive
  Vice President, ————
  Past President, ————

- National Housing Services
  Member of the Board, Benton Park, and Soulard Neighborhoods

- ———— Political Action Committee
  Past Member of the Contributions Committee

- ———— Women's Network
  Founding Member, Member of the Board

- ———— Women's Commerce Association
  Former Board Trustee, Founder of the Boardroom Breakfast

Other Interests

Investment in and renovation of multiple-family housing. Sailing, both racing and cruising.

tinctions and honors she had received during her career. What she lacked in "formal" credentials, she made up for in community involvement and recognition.

The final section was added to highlight the close relationship between her career interests and her personal life, including a statement about her investment in and renovation of multiple-family housing.

Now you are in for a real treat. Meet Jack, large build, ready smile, devoted to his family and friends, and highly proficient in industrial-engineering–related skills. His particular areas of expertise and areas of greatest pride included facilities layout and design, production methods and operation, and warehouse handling/warehousing. His résumé represents eighteen years with a company, a great deal of growth and participation in company goals and objectives, and a large number of accomplishments over this period of time. In addition to developing a functional résumé organized by areas of effectiveness (see exhibit C), Jack decided to develop another support sheet which would highlight alternative professional goals and summarize specific project involvement (see exhibit D). As he was developing this sheet, he was reminded of his high-level communication skills, his interest in employee communication, and his orientation toward issues relating to the quality of work life.

By evaluating and summarizing his project work, Jack isolated a variety of alternative targets for himself, including materials handling/facilities planning, human resource development, manpower planning, quality of work life, quality circles, and organizational development. These professional orientations broadened his search to include positions that were tangentially related to his previous work experience.

Jack's résumé, which he used for positions that would draw on his experience in facilities layout and design, production methods and operation, and materials handling/warehousing, concluded with a Summary of Interests and Affiliations. He listed several areas of interest which were deeply important to him, including involvement in marriage encounter, sailing, and restoration of old homes. He

Exhibit C
JACK DOBSON
Address
Phone

Professional Objective

Management position in materials handling or facilities planning for a manufacturing, distribution, or warehousing operation. A position requiring someone with creative problem-solving talents; responsive management style; and ability to develop, motivate, and work effectively with people of diverse orientations.

Professional Experience

Facilities Layout & Design

- Developed overall plan for a 100,000-square-foot, roughly a 50% increase, addition to main manufacturing facility. Plan based on overall material-handling concept and each department's need to interact with warehouse facilities.

- Supervised layout, planning, and coordination of move of fourteen production departments, meeting overall target dates of plans extending over fourteen-month period.

- Redesigned the machine assembly methods, laid out new floor plan, and coordinated the relocation of the machine assembly department. Changes resulted in the doubling of capacity and an increase in productivity of approximately 15%.

Production Methods & Operation

- Managed the creation of a central tool crib to service all production departments. Evaluated the storage and service needs of each department; developed a storage and service system to meet these needs. A very efficient tool management system was developed to control a tooling budget of over $1 million, through the successful coordination of Tool Engineering, MIS, Production Supervisory personnel, and a computerized inventory system.

• Developed manufacturing method for new machines to be completely assembled and packaged at subcontractor's plant. Negotiated with subcontractor and instructed his employees about assembly techniques. Worked with product development department to modify design of product so that greater volume could be loaded in each trailer, reducing transportation cost by 50%.

• Eliminated the use of wood crates by substituting triple-wall corrugated containers, thereby saving $80,000 annually. Also developed systems to transport, warehouse, and handle these large, knocked-down containers from supplier to remote warehouse, then to packing department.

Materials Handling/ Warehousing

• Managed the design, equipment selection, installation, and start-up of a four-aisle, man-aboard, storage and order-picking system 35 feet high and 120 feet long, handling 6,000 items. Project was completed on time and within the $400,000 budget.

• Managed the redesign of a 24,000-square-foot, high-rise, very narrow-aisle parts and assembly warehouse. Engineered all equipment and vehicles. Coordinated installation of new equipment and movement of existing ware with only minor disruption ofwarehousing operation. Increased usable cubage by 30% within existing building and throughout potential by almost 50%.

• Supervised the relocation of raw materials stores operation. Selected additional equipment to increase storage capacity by 50%. Coordinated and supervised the installation of old and new equipment as well as the 1,500,000 lbs. of stock on hand. With the aid of computer printouts and conversion programs supplied by MIS, completed installation, move, and physical inventory in less than three months with no disruption in service.

JACK DOBSON
Phone
Page Three

- Planned and organized intermediate move of shipping department and finished goods stores, permitting continuing operation during construction period. Completed the movement of stock of over 6,000 items over a three-day weekend to insure continued effective customer service.

- Planned and organized the relocation of a small-parts storage operation involving 12,000 part numbers, after first designing the new layout and operation methods. Move was accomplished on time in a manner which permitted the continued operation of the warehouse.

- Developed an in-process storage, retrieval, and delivery system which reduced the use of manufacturing floor space for storage by 8,000 square feet. By organizing and recording placement of parts, drastically reduced time spent by production workers searching for parts, thereby promoting closer adherance to production schedules.

- Conceived and implemented a system of free stock and run modules to streamline the logistics, record keeping, handling, and issuing of small parts to the assembly departments.

Educational/ Professional Development

B.S., Industrial Management, Washington University, St. Louis, Missouri, 1970

Numerous Courses including:

Supervisory Skills Training Program, Counseling Skills Training Program, Discipline Without Punishment, Assertive Management, Time Management, Modern Supervisor, Working with People, Management by Objectives.

Productivity Possibilities, Materials Handling for the '80s, Preventive Maintenance, Organic Coating Applications.

JACK DOBSON
Phone
Page Four

Employment History

————, St. Louis, Missouri	1965–present
Manufacturing Engineer	1981–present
Supervisor of Industrial Engineering	1978–1981
Supervisor of Production Engineering	1974–1978
Production Engineer	1970–1974
NC Engineer/Programmer, Tool Engineer/Designer	1967–1970
————, St. Louis, Missouri	1957–1965

Machinist, Tool Maker/Apprentice
Metallurgical Lab Technician, Work Order Clerk

Summary of Interests & Affiliations

- Participant in worldwide marriage encounter organization
- Avid small-boat and sailing enthusiast
- Challenged by restoration and preservation of craftsmanship of old homes
- Member of:
  - American Institute of Industrial Engineers
  - Society of Packaging and Handling Engineers
  - Packaging Institute

Exhibit D
JACK DOBSON
Address
Phone

Professional Goals

A leadership position in an organization committed to achieving organizational goals by helping employees maximize their contributions by developing their individual potential.

A position where my considerable and varied industrial engineering experience and effective interpersonal skills can be applied. This position would direct or participate in emerging programs related to the development of human potential, implemented under the auspices of departments such as:

Quality of work life
Quality circles
Human resource development
Organizational development
Manpower planning

Summary of Related Project Involvement

Summary of related project involvement and techniques used to improve results through employee participation:

- Converted finished goods stores and order-picking operations to a four-aisle, man-aboard system and developed computer support.
  - —Brainstorming with employees
  - —Mutual goal setting
  - —Reality testing with employees

- Developed interrelated layouts for fourteen manufacturing departments and coordinated their relocation.
  - —Open two-way communications
  - —Assisting in needs assessment
  - —Publicizing progress reports

JACK DOBSON
Phone
Page Two

- Managed the creation of a central tool crib to service all manufacturing departments.
  - —Cause-and-effect problem solving
  - —Stressing job enrichment
  - —Assistance in needs assessment
- Reorganized and rearranged the machine assembly department to increase capacity and efficiency by improving methods.
  - —Team problem-identification sessions
  - —Process cause-and-effect problem analysis
  - —Definition of objectives
- Designed a new, small-parts warehouse operation to improve cube utilization, record accuracy, and efficiency.
  - —Problem identification
  - —Employee-generated data
  - —Concept evaluation

believed that including this information would provide an opening for meaningful connecting at the beginning of a meeting.

The additional support sheet Jack developed allowed him to summarize his specific project involvement. It was headed by a statement of his professional goals, and included a summary of project involvement used to improve bottom-line results through employee participation. When exploring options tangentially related to his previous position, he used this sheet as a stimulus to conversation and a reflection of his past. He also used it in combination with a detailed letter when responding to ads for positions that he believed he could do well but for which he did not have the directly requested credentials.

Enter Tony, a multitalented individual who had worked successfully in both the profit and not-for-profit sectors. His most recent position was as director of sales for a national network of sales reps working for a manufacturing and distribution company. Prior to this position, Tony had been the director of a social service agency for eight years. And prior to that position he had been in the profit sector in a number of capacities, including sales, marketing, technical, and manufacturing positions.

What was exciting about working with Tony was his openness to exploring a diversity of scenarios simultaneously. He could picture himself in positions similar to some of his previous ones, as well as ones he had not previously considered. Tony decided that the best way for him to market himself was to create a different résumé for each different job target. He isolated several job categories to explore, including the vice president of human resources; vice president of sales; executive director of an agency; and consultant for sales, marketing, human resources, training, manufacturing, planning, or organizational development.

Tony believed that he could best take advantage of his broad-based experience through individual résumés that listed the target at the top, followed by his capabilities that related to that target, and concluding with his accomplishments that related specifically to that target. Each résumé ended with a list of job titles and employers and a description of his educational background. (See exhibits E and F.)

This résumé format worked extremely well for Tony. He was very focused at each meeting, choosing the relevant résumé to use to reflect his credentials. People with whom he interviewed did not have to look at information not related to their specific need, and Tony always had the latitude to give further information about his background and experience when asked.

With these résumés Tony could focus his audience on only what was relevant from his background and experience to the discussion at hand. He could eliminate, for the moment, extraneous information that might confuse the reader or send unclear messages about his strengths and abilities. Each time Tony developed a new target scenario, he developed a new format for his résumé. Tony ended up directing a not-for-profit agency in his next position, and he looks back on his job-search experience as a tremendously upbeat, educational learning experience for himself.

Exhibit E
TONY BASTION
Address
Phone

Job Target: Executive Director

Capabilities:

* Manage a large staff with simultaneous projects
* Develop plan and management by objectives system
* Develop and motivate teams
* Organize and implement fund-raising plan
* Make effective presentations to prospective donors
* Establish and implement program evaluation
* Understand and implement programmatic issues
* Work for and maintain effective volunteer board
* Attract competent board members
* Market and sell products and services
* Develop effective marketing tools for new and existing products

Accomplishments:

* Took three organizations through management by objectives and long-range planning process
* Adjunct professor with highest marks as graduate teacher of human resource management and contemporary management techniques
* Successfully took agency through its first accreditation by The Joint Commission on Accreditation of Hospitals
* Reduced turnover from 90% to 20%
* Developed budgeting systems for $50 million, $10 million, and $500,000 companies
* Saved $1 million by teaching employees about operations improvement
* Vice president of the ———— chapter of the National Society of Fund-Raising Executives
* Increased client fees threefold
* Chairman of Children's Services panel for ————

TONY BASTION
Phone
Page Two

* Edited book ———
* Board of Directors, American Association of Psychiatric Services for Children
* Developed child sexual-abuse treatment program
* Set up evaluation system for outpatient psychiatric clinic
* President of ten volunteer boards
* Board trainer for ———
* Developed and implemented marketing strategy that caused threefold increase in clients
* Doubled growth rate of $10 million chemical company
* Won outstanding marketing bonus and was youngest salesman to be promoted to senior salesman

Exhibit F
TONY BASTION
Address
Phone

Job Target: Vice President of Sales

Capabilities:

* Build a winning and fun sales team
* Develop and meet sales forecasts
* Manage and develop products and markets
* Understand the selling and marketing function
* Manage, lead, and direct a sales force
* Develop new product campaigns including sales promotion literature, advertising, training, and market research
* Recruit and train a sales force
* Understand customers
* Sell

TONY BASTION
Phone
Page Two

Accomplishments:

* Directed a sales force of 25, whereby sales growth doubled for 2 consecutive years
* Managed four field sales managers, advertising, promotion, and marketing services departments
* Guided growth of new product line to top selling in company
* Increased sales 500% in two years
* Developed the marketing and sales plan for a new product whose sales doubled forecast
* Promoted to youngest senior salesman in company
* Won outstanding marketing employee bonus
* Redesigned hiring standards, recruiting, and training
* Reduced sales turnover from 90% to 20%
* Redesigned sales compensation system
* Developed management by objectives and customer strategy system

Experience:

1986–Present	Director of Sales
1976–1986	Executive Director
1972–1976	Director of Admin.
	Assistant to Pres. &
	Corporate Sec.

Finally we'd like you to meet Marc, a thoughtful, incisive thinker with deep commitment to contributing to the world in ways that felt significant to him. His two previous positions were as executive director to two different residential agencies working with abused and neglected children. Prior to that, Marc was a university psychology instructor. His degree was a doctorate in counseling and educational psychology.

When Marc was fired, he took the time to think broadly about the possible application of the expertise he had developed. Up until working with us, he had concluded that his career would be in the not-for-profit sector or possibly in management in a college setting. He began to think more broadly about possibilities for himself.

The scenarios he considered for himself included the following list:

- Director of an agency
- Dean of a college
- President of small college
- Development director of college
- Philanthropy director
- Director of corporate responsibility
- Full-time lobbyist
- Consultant to not-for-profits
- Second in command or right-hand person to president of small- or medium-size company
- Ministry work

Marc's areas of effectiveness were congruent with the talents needed for each of the above scenarios and included the following:

- Strategic/Corporate planning
- Community leadership
- Financial management
- Legislative/Political relations
- Lobbying
- Development/Fund-raising/Philanthropy
- Refounding/Resurrecting organizations
- Board expertise/Community leadership
- Grantsmanship
- New program design implementation
- Organizational management/Leadership
- Labor relations/Personnel practices

Since Marc had so many strong community contacts, he knew that he wouldn't be doing any mass mailings, and would be hand-delivering every résumé that he used. Therefore he decided to put together an expanded résumé format, using separate pages to address each of four areas of effectiveness that he felt provided the very core of his strengths and talents (see exhibit G for one page of his résumé). The four areas included: Refounding Organizations/Development/Grantsmanship; Strategic/Corporate Planning; Board Expertise/Community Leadership; and Legislative or Political Relationships/Lobbying.

Marc concluded his packet with a list of employment experience and education. Since he had separate sheets relating his accomplishments by areas of effectiveness, Marc could utilize the sheets that addressed a particular target, and eliminate those that were irrelevant. He included the sheet on church leadership only when interviewing for positions where it would be highly relevant. Marc's job search concluded in his working first as a director of a not-for-profit agency. He eventually joined a consulting company that specialized in consulting for the not-for-profit sector, relocating his family for this outstanding opportunity.

We hope that meeting our client/friends has given you an inside look into the thinking behind the evolution of a résumé. You may have been surprised, however, that the résumé samples we have shown you extend beyond one page. Many résumé experts emphasize the need to be brief and limit résumés to one page.

We agree with the need to organize the information so that the reader has an overall understanding of the potential contribution of the job searcher. Some résumés that have been ill conceived ramble on unncessarily and could well be condensed.

Nonetheless, our experience with middle and upper management individuals whose experience covers ten to twenty successful years is that they may need to capture the breadth and scope of their accomplishments on more than one page. This works only if the résumé is carefully planned and created. We hope to show you how to develop a résumé that will competently represent your accomplishments.

Exhibit G
MARC LANDING
Address
Phone

Refounding Organizations/Development/Grantsmanship

- As Executive Director of residential agency providing emergency shelter and treatment services, diversified services, overcame significant deficit, established income stream, and increased net worth by 60% in five years, to more than $4 million.

- As Executive Director of agency that operates a school for 110 developmentally disabled children and 80 adults, identified and secured new monies through development of new federal grants and negotiating increases in present schedules with the Department of Elementary and Secondary Education. Worked closely with the Department of Mental Health to develop community programs, resulting in $1 million/year in continuing monies for new programs.

- Developed strategies to secure crucial funding for unique program for profoundly retarded individuals through negotiation with the Department of Elementary and Secondary Education. Directed grant toward the nonsectarian school associated with the agency and released funds that had been impounded.

- Spearheaded and negotiated for significant expansion of an initial $29,000 grant for deaf-blind youngsters to a $100,000 yearly grant through identification of new monies available from the state.

- Led successful $1,300,000 fund drive from community corporate sources, resulting in increased agency revenue and improved reputation in the community.

- Secured $½ million from the Department of Mental Health to expand pilot project to off-campus program that continues 8 years later. Placed several clients who had not originally even qualified for a sheltered workshop into competitive employment.

MARC LANDING
Phone
Page Two

- Significantly increased revenue base by decreasing number of clients not reimbursed. Resulted in new balance of funded and unfunded programs, providing the agency with a solid financial base.

- Supervised design and construction of $1,000,000 facility, including new school and recreation building. Resulted in significantly updated campus and increased qualifications for program reimbursement.

- Defined and negotiated new reporting procedures and methods of collection for state reimbursement, resulting in a 40% ($220,000) increase in revenue in the first three-month period.

Following are a set of stimulus questions that can get you started thinking about what résumé format would best serve you:

- Do you want a chronological or functional résumé or a combined format? Which would best do you justice? (Anytime you are thinking about a career shift you would find a functional résumé more helpful and less restrictive.)
- Do you want to begin your résumé with a specific target statement, or would you prefer a personal or professional summary—or both? (If you are a controller and want to be a controller, a target statement is advisable. If you are a controller and want to consider financial planning, becoming a stockbroker or a senior lending officer in a financial institution, a summary would work better.)
- Do you want to begin your résumé with a list of qualifications, to provide a frame for the reader? Would you like to begin it with a list of areas of potential contribution, to focus the reader on options?
- Do you want to do a different résumé for each different job you are targeting? (In some ways it is simpler, and it does focus

the reader, marketing you explicitly into a distinct job category.)

- Do you want to do a longer format—several sheets in a binder? (Will you be doing a very individualized job search primarily through networking, bringing your résumé with you to leave behind?)
- Are there additional sheets you can create which will help you market yourself more effectively than just using a résumé? Ask yourself, "How can I summarize my talents in a different way?" (For example, if you are good at strategic planning and are targeting consulting, make a list of all the different strategic planning projects in which you have been involved during your career. Use that sheet instead of a résumé.)

Preparing to Write Your Résumé Using the Mind-Mapping Process

Writing your résumé can be fun. *No kidding.* But if you are like most of our clients, you will have some resistance to the process. Even people who write easily tend to avoid writing résumés. As a matter of fact, our worst clients (in terms of résumé writing) have been human resource managers or writers, those who you would assume would be the best.

We've heard many stories about writers' resistance to writing. Successful, prolific writers often have difficulty with the self-discipline writing requires. One famous writer admitted tying himself to his desk chair in his underwear each day to prevent himself from the inevitable excuse to "take a break."

Since you will, however, have to write a résumé, some letters, a proposal or two, summaries for a portfolio, we'd like to make writing easier for you than possibly it has been in the past. We'd like to teach you a new skill—mind mapping.

In chapter 1 we introduced you to your brain by sharing with you the exciting new information we now have about the brain. You recall that the left side of your brain is thought to be linear, logical, and rational and the right side is more imaginative, free flowing, intuitive, making patterns and connections for you. Well, your left side is usually in charge when you need to write a report or summarize a project or develop a presentation. If you are like most of us, when you were in grammar school, you were taught outlining and linear notetaking. Using these techniques, you established a plan for any writing project, and you developed your text from that plan.

The problem with approaching a task in this way is that your right brain does not actually work best in outline, linear form. It works best if allowed to spill its ideas out onto a sheet of paper, look at them, add to them, and expand them. The organizing comes later—when you want to determine an order and a specific focus. In this way, you are using both sides of your brain, your whole brain, and in doing so, you more effortlessly arrive at higher-quality writing. Fortunately, a process has been developed to achieve such a purpose: mind mapping.

Mind mapping was originally developed in the early 1970s by British author and brain researcher Tony Buzan, and it was further developed and applied in numerous creative ways by Michael Gelb. Mind mapping is a nonlinear method of representing your ideas in which you may decide to use key words, color (to highlight ideas), and visual images (either simple or, if you are comfortable drawing pictures, complex).

Michael Gelb describes this process extremely well in *Present Yourself!* (Jalmar Press, 1988), one of the best books on developing presentations that has been published. Gelb has worked with key executives in major corporations throughout the United States, teaching them mind mapping and then using it to develop everything from presentations to five-year strategic plans.

By using mind mapping to plan the writing of your résumé (or any other piece, for that matter), you can more easily capture numerous ideas that demonstrate obvious interconnections, and establish a pattern that will communicate more effectively to your audience. We'll show you what we mean.

We'll walk you through your first mind map. Take out a large piece of unlined blank paper and a number of colored pens. You may want to put some baroque music on in the background. The subject of this mind map will be your accomplishments throughout your career—by area of expertise.

Draw an image in the center of the paper. It can be anything which relates to your career. If you have been a manager in a beer company, you could draw a can of beer. If you have been an architect, you may decide to draw an outline of a building. If you have been the director of the Heart Foundation, you might draw a heart. Any image will do. (Don't worry if your image is recognizable only to you; the plan is only for your eyes!)

Next, focus on key words. When you think of areas of effectiveness, areas of expertise, what comes to mind? If you are the director of the Heart Foundation, you may first think of raising money. Draw a line radiating out from your image and write in all capital letters the word MONEY or just $$$. Use only one word to represent an idea. Your brain will remember what it stands for. What comes to mind next? Perhaps public relations or marketing efforts come to mind. Choose another color and draw another line from the image and write PR or MARKETING on it. Now, allow your brain to wander through your other thoughts. What else were you effective in doing? Perhaps you are especially skilled in hiring and training. If so, draw another line (again with a different color) and write EMPLOYMENT or HIRING on it. And so on.

By the time you have allowed all your ideas to spill out, you will have a central image with many lines radiating out from it, each with one word or one picture on it.

At any point you can go back to any of the lines radiating out from your image and invite your mind to wander in that area. It is important not to force the ideas but merely to allow them to evolve while you are free associating. How can you expand that thought? What other thoughts come to mind? How can you describe it further or make it more specific? Radiating from EMPLOYMENT could be several lines—including HIRING, FIRING, LEGAL, INTERVIEWS, TURNOVER, etc. Each word is on a separate line and printed in capital letters. If you can easily think of an image or a symbol instead of the word, use it. Your brain *loves* pictures and images and remembers them more easily than words.

Once you have allowed all of your thoughts to be transferred to paper, you have a multicolored, nonlinear, symbol- and image-rich mind map. And you probably even enjoyed creating it. Now you can begin to think about the order of importance, how one entry may actually be a subset of another, which ones to omit. Often the organization will naturally follow just from looking at the various segments of the map, and you can number them or draw arrows from one to another to indicate relationships.

As we move through each stage of constructing a résumé, try mind-mapping your thoughts before organizing them. You'll find that writing becomes almost effortless, and your résumé and letters will write themselves.

Here is a completed version of the mind map for our mythical director of the Heart Foundation:

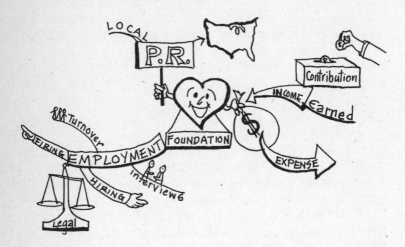

Looking over this mind map, you will see some patterns emerging. You will have a much better idea of how the areas of expertise interface with each other. If you were to come back to this diagram at a later date, after you had done some more thinking about your background, you might have some additional information to insert. It will be easy to do so with this brainstorming tool, because the information you need for your résumé is laid out in front of you on one page, in an easily accessible form. Like the blueprint for a building, the mind map provides you with a visual plan for your written résumé.

Constructing Your Résumé

Step One

What are the scenarios or job targets that you would like this résumé to address? Make a mind map of your options with a picture of you in the center. As you record each possibility radiating from the central image, others may occur to you. Perhaps you are a marketing manager. You might put yourself at the center and have lines radiating from that center with the words MARKETING, RESEARCH, COMMUNICATIONS, MARKETING RESEARCH indicating the various positions that would be a good fit for your talents and experience base.

Step Two

If you take a moment to glance at the résumés earlier in the chapter, you will notice that the bulleted items are all accomplishment oriented. Through these items you will tell a story about your expertise. The best way for you to get in touch with your accomplishments is to think of your experience in terms of *problems, actions,* and *results.*

In any given situation what were the problems with which you were dealing? What actions did you take in order to solve those problems? What resulted from the actions you took, either alone or as part of a team? How did each accomplishment change your job, your perception of yourself, the way you were perceived by others, or your future capabilities?

Before you make your own comprehensive list of problems, actions, and results, let's define what we mean by "problem." What we do *not* mean is something that went wrong. Rather, we are using the word *problem* in a neutral sense—a *challenge* or *activity* or *unmet need* or *purpose* that was your responsibility individually or as part of a team or group. Every job is made up of a series of activities and challenges and goals that need addressing. At each different stage in your career, what were they for you?

When creating a list of problems, actions, and results, don't forget to include what you have done and accomplished as a volunteer or in an avocation. Running a Sunday school, serving on an advisory board of family and children's services, or planning all programs of the American Marketing Association should definitely be on your list. Don't censor anything that comes to mind. One woman wryly admitted that her best accomplishment had to do with moving eight times in fourteen years with her husband, who was constantly being transferred. Though said in jest, that "small" problem that she dealt with most expertly formed the core of one of her primary targets: working as a relocation counselor in a company specializing in relocation services.

It is likely that you will be hired because of the perception that you can solve problems or satisfy unmet needs, so the list you create will be useful to you in many ways. In addition to pinpointing the accomplishments for your résumé and your letters, it will help you when discussing the contributions you might make to an organization. You could see a job interview or exploratory meeting as an opportunity to find out whether challenges match your problem-solving experience.

Following is a stimulus list of problems, actions, and results to trigger your memory. After glancing at this list, mind-map your own problems/activities/goals. Then you can make a list from your mind map. For example, if you have been running companies, your mind map might include a central image of an executive desk. Radiating from the center could be categories of problems you've handled. You might include GROWTH MANAGEMENT, NEW PRODUCT/SERVICE DEVELOPMENT, EMPLOYEE MOTIVATION, COST CUTTING, PLANT/WAREHOUSE DEVELOPMENT, INCENTIVE PLANS, COMPETITION, etc. Within each of these categories might be any number of specific problems you remember. Here is a sample list:

Problems/Actions/Results

Increasing costs
Decreasing sales
Decreasing profits
Escalating employee costs
Escalating insurance costs

Inefficiency of interdepartmental communication
Decreasing morale
Cumbersome work flow
Slow delivery and follow-through
Decreased productivity

Increasing pressure from financial backers
Decreasing influence in the marketplace
Increasing loss of accounts to competitors
Lack of appropriate information about accounts
Ineffective computer system

Too many back orders
Lack of government support
Poor packaging
Decreasing quality of interaction with customer
Loss of market share and need for alternative products

Increasing technology/decreasing employee competence
Increase in utility costs
Lack of managerial effectiveness
Lack of employee commitment to details
Bad public image

Decreased salespersons' motivation
Waste of time by administrative staff
Lack of commitment to excellence
Reliance on outside sales/need for telemarketing
Lack of adequate training programs

Lack of high-level brainstorming/interchange
Increasing legal costs
Increasing recruiting costs
Increasing affirmative-action lawsuits
Inadequate strategic planning

Increasing cost of raw materials
Increasing demands by consumers for service
Refusal of employees to accept promotions or transfers
Increasing need to consolidate and downsize
Increase in safety problems.

Unclear goals and objectives
Authoritarian atmosphere that prevents employee participation
Unequal opportunities for minorities
Lack of child-care facilities
High stress and high employee turnover

Strong competition for corporate dollars
Bad community relationships
Inadequate advertising and public relations
Static perception of employee capabilities
Shrinking market share

Step Three

After you have completed your list of problems, actions, and results, you can put them in résumé language. Look at some of the résumé samples in this chapter. Notice three things about the accomplishments that are listed. First, they begin with a strong verb. Second, they quantify what you did in terms of dollars, numbers, and percentages whenever possible. Third, they often end in a result, which answers the question "So what?" In other words, *why* are you telling the reader that you put in place a five-year strategic plan? What was the impact, the result?

Take your list of problems, actions, and results and use a dictionary or thesaurus to find action verbs to help you rewrite your statements in accomplishment form. Your list will be longer than you can include on a résumé, but save the extra statements. Any examples not used in your résumé will be useful later when you are writing letters, proposals, or planning for effective meetings.

Step Four

Now it's time to choose what type of résumé will work best for you. We've presented several chronological, functional, combined, individualized by target, longer format in a binder—or you can develop some creation of your own.

If you choose a functional résumé, you can begin to rough out the areas of effectiveness that will divide your résumé. After you choose three to five specific areas of expertise, you can pull examples from throughout your work experience to support each section. The chronological résumé will list your previous employers throughout the body of the résumé, whereas the functional résumé will call for a work history after the areas of effectiveness. Remember—the functional résumé is best used when shifting focus or moving in new directions, when you've had many job changes, or when you are targeting positions for which you believe you are qualified but don't have proof in the traditional sense.

Whichever format you choose, chronological or functional, al-

ways start your work history with the most recent job or company
affiliation and work backward, as in the sample résumés. It's
legitimate to list your last job as "to present" even if you were fired.
It won't be interpreted as being dishonest and is standard format.

It is important to be scrupulous in listing where you have worked
and the exact years in each position. In many states there are strict
requirements for employers to check out the previous work
histories of job applicants, partly due to newly evolving negligent-
hiring laws. These laws hold an employer responsible for the
actions of employees they have hired. They'll want absolute proof
about gaps in your work history. If you took a year out to travel or
a few years out to raise children or time out to get a degree,
proudly list it in the work experience section.

Step Five

For the concluding sections of the résumé, you will need information on education and training, certification, associations and
organizations to which you belong, special interests relevant to
your job search, and personal dimensions beyond your work history
that might enhance your job search.

Begin with your formal education. List your degrees and special
areas of study, research, or advanced learning. List names and
dates of seminars and courses taken, including in-house courses. If
you are working toward a degree, state "currently working toward
degree in public administration; completion date, 1992." State your
most recent formal education first and work backward. Next, list
specialized courses, working from current to the least recent.

The final section of your résumé can be called Special Interests;
Interests/Affiliations; Personal Interests Beyond Work History;
Interests/Publications; Professional/Community Affiliations; Re-
lated Achievements; Personal; or any other title of your choosing.
Make a mind map about what is special about you to help you here.
What is unique? What would make you stand out? What does the
body of the résumé not adequately address?

Include in this section whatever you consider important or

indicative of the type of person you are. Here you might state that you are a few hours from receiving your pilot's license, or that you are an avid photographer or a fitness enthusiast. Whatever you put here could very well stimulate interesting conversation with your interviewer and set a positive tone for the meeting.

This last section of your résumé provides an opportunity for you to personalize. Experiment—look for ways for the résumé to stimulate interest and reflect your individuality. Resist the temptation to state whether you are married, how many children you have, how old they are, your height and weight, or to include a picture. Such data is outmoded and strictly illegal to request. Let them judge you on your qualifications, not your marital status. (If you have specific information that a company you are targeting prefers to hire family men, for example, then you might want to individualize a résumé and include this information for that one target.)

Be careful also about including information about organizations that could be perceived as threatening to those who will be reading your résumé. If you are a president of the local chapter of NOW (National Organization for Women), you may want to state that you are president of a women's organization. Or if you are holding office in your church, you may want to leave off the name or the affiliation of the church so that you will not trigger stereotyped or prejudiced reactions from your interviewer.

Step Six

Like the roof of a house, the objective or professional summary is of obvious importance—but is written last. Just as a builder investigates the plans thoroughly prior to building and knows what materials he will use for the roof prior to construction, the objective or professional summary must be carefully thought out prior to development of the résumé. The actual wording, the particular emphasis and thrust are created after completion of the draft.

There are various ways to open your résumé, depending on your job objectives.

Specific Targeted Statement (often stated as "Objective")

If you are a human resources professional targeting a position in human resources, with responsibility for hiring, benefits, wage and salary administration, union negotiations, and safety, then say so in the objective:

> Director of Human Resources with responsibility for hiring, benefits, wage and salary administration, union negotiations, and safety

No need to say any more. Your job search is confined to that target; your objective should be straightforward.

An Expanded Targeted Statement

You state what position you are targeting, but enlarge on it to expand on your qualifications and paint a broader picture of your background and expertise:

> Vice President/Director of Management Information Systems or equivalent MIS management position

- Have proven expertise in information systems, telecommunications, distributed systems, computer operations, and development of MIS plans supportive of business objectives.
- Special talent in deemphasizing technological mystique and emphasizing use of MIS to have positive impact on the bottom line.

Statement of Areas of Potential Contribution

This will focus the reader and project you into his company's *future* rather than only reflecting on your *past*. Here is an example:

- Design and develop technical and managerial training programs for all MIS personnel.
- Design, create, and implement career development program for MIS personnel.
- Develop, implement, support the Information Center concept to serve as interface to users of DP, using variety of

techniques to facilitate use of computer by noncomputer professionals.

- Develop and install comprehensive user-training program for purchasers of personal computers in home and business environment.
- Assess needs and develop individualized productivity improvement workshops.

Each of the above potential areas of contribution is a kernel of a possible job objective, and each represents one or more areas of expertise.

Professional Summary

If the above MIS manager preferred to summarize his background rather than target a job objective, the following description would be a viable alternative:

Manager with high-level technical knowledge and skills in data processing and management development training . . . qualified by 25 years on the cutting edge of the computer revolution . . . demonstrated success in designing and implementing technical, management development, and career development training for MIS personnel . . . proven talent in needs assessment to determine which problems are amenable to computer solution and to provide services to user groups . . . special talent in working with non–computer-trained individuals and in demystifying technological mystique.

Following is another example of a professional summary that focuses the reader and organizes his background and experience in a few sentences:

Manager of Maintenance Services and Production/Engineering, or Maintenance and Facilities Engineer.

Special expertise in the following areas:

- Developing machinery, often in conjunction with new products.
- Redesigning troublesome processes, troubleshooting.
- Supervising contracts on the job.
- Initiating and developing apprenticeship programs.
- Researching and developing methods to make repairs or replace machinery at the lowest possible cost.
- Technical skills, including welding, sheet metal work, machine shop, electrical, plumbing, carpentry, roofing, cabinetmaking, auto repair, auto body repair, machine rebuilding, materials specification for proper repairs, remodeling, appliance repairs, specialized equipment design, metallurgy, rebuilding tractors, installation of equipment.

Highlights of Qualifications

The final method of starting your résumé can be just a few bulleted statements, summarizing the highlights of your background and experience for the reader:

- More than 15 years' experience in education, career planning, and job-search advisement.
- Master's degree and considerable relevant postgraduate training in areas related to lifelong learning.
- Proven ability in providing guidance and motivation to enable clients and students to establish and meet career goals.
- Future oriented; capable of providing cutting edge information.

This short list provides a focused picture of the candidate—before the reader gets to the body of the résumé.

One last detail in preparing your résumé is to consider your name, address, and telephone number. These will appear, of course, at the top of the first page. You'll want to put your name and phone number on the top of each of the succeeding pages as well.

The telephone number you will be using will depend on who will be answering your calls. Over the years our clients have found the best alternatives are to use their home phone number, using a quality answering machine, or sign up with an answering service during their job search so that their telephone will be professionally covered when they are out. In most circumstances, calls can be forwarded to the answering service by pushing one or more buttons on the phone. Check with your local telephone company and answering service companies to find out what will work for you.

After You Have Written Your Résumé, What Do You Do with It?

By now we've made our biases clear. Don't throw together a résumé that doesn't effectively communicate who you are and what you can contribute. Invest in the time and careful thought to do it well. Make sure that you either have it word-processed in a quality manner, with headings entered in bold print, or have your résumé typeset. Typesetting is no longer necessary because of sophisticated word-processing and desktop publishing programs.

The advantage of word-processing your résumé (as opposed to doing it on a traditional typewriter) is that you'll have a final copy that is polished and will permit more words in less space. If you have had a long, successful career, as many of our clients have, you might choose to print your résumé in a booklet form that ends up as a monarch-size sheet when folded over. Page one opens up to pages two and three. This three-page format is really one large sheet folded in half.

The disadvantage of a typeset résumé (as opposed to getting one word-processed) is that once you have it printed, you must live with it. If you change your mind and want it different in some way, you'll have to have it typeset again at tremendous expense.

You'll want the stationery you use for your résumé to match the stationery you are using for your cover letter. Purchase top-grade bond paper in a neutral color such as white, off-white, or light gray.

Be certain that whoever types the final version of your résumé, whether it is typeset or word-processed, has eliminated any grammatical or typographical errors. You'd be surprised how these can escape the most seasoned proofreaders.

One client, Karen, printed up hundreds of résumés only to realize that her telephone number had been incorrectly listed. Having caught the error after less than twenty résumés had been mailed out, Karen called the number mistakenly listed on her résumé and chatted with a friendly woman at the other end. She couldn't understand why the woman on the other end was being so friendly, until she told Karen that her husband had recently sent out résumés targeting a position in public administration—but accidentally eliminated the *l* in *public!* She would gladly refer any calls to Karen from the first batch of résumés.

How to Use Your Résumé

There may be many occasions when you will have no choice but to send your résumé ahead of you. A headhunter wants one—you comply with their request. A want ad lists only a box number, but the ad sounds intriguing—you forward your résumé. You decide to do a limited mailing—researching the name of the person to whom you would report in each company—and forward your résumé to those persons.

Whenever possible during your job search, hand-deliver your résumé at the time of the meeting. Leave it behind, but try not to send it ahead. Does that sound blasphemous—to try and avoid sending a résumé ahead when someone specifically requested one? We don't think it is so outrageous.

So how can you avoid sending a résumé ahead prior to a meeting? If you are introduced to someone through a friend, you can ask the friend making the introductory call to pass on as much information about you as possible. That might preclude even being asked for a résumé, just as it would have a year ago when you were not out looking.

If you are asked to forward a résumé and you are just setting up a meeting to explore industry possibilities, you can say that you are not applying for a position, but rather approaching them for their counsel. Therefore a résumé would not be appropriate at this point. Or you can say that you are in the process of developing a résumé that will accurately reflect your background and experience, and you intend to bring it along with you to the meeting. Your goal is, whenever possible, to have them meet the three-dimensional you prior to seeing your résumé.

The Second Dimension—Letter Writing and Proposals

Letter writing should never be done perfunctorily. Rather, your letters should have energy, focus, and an obvious reason for being sent. Alone, a letter will not necessarily reap results. Writing letters could be compared to gathering wood for a fire and preparing to send up smoke signals to those out there who need and want your special expertise and experience. It is a prelude or a follow-up to meetings. But it is often a necessary first step. Letters can kindle or reactivate interests or maintain momentum. They are smoke signals that make up meaningful exchange and can lead to employment.

In Response to an Advertisement

Admit it—you *are* reading want ads! No matter what all the job-search gurus say about ads only representing a tiny percentage of the job opportunities, you can't shake the belief that the want ads are the first place to go. We'll let you in on a secret. Even outplacement and job-search counselors, when considering a job change, go first to the want ads. After all, it would be so easy if that would lead to the perfect job. And it *has* been known to happen.

If you're going to read and answer ads anyway, we'll show you one of the more successful ways to respond to ads. Our clients have had success with a letter format that has the position criteria from the ad listed down on the left side of the page and specific accomplishments or knowledge from your background and experience listed to the right.

The following example is from an architect who had spent his entire career in a corporation. The ad read:

Architectural Project Manager, with minimum of seven years experience in each of the following areas: Renovation design, project management, leadership, design-engineering consulting, project cost control, design critique, and project coordination/liaison.

A portion of his letter is reproduced below:

October 9, 1988

Hotels Corporation
Chicago, Illinois 60680

Gentlemen:
In response to your *Chicago Tribune* advertisement for an Architectural Project Manager, I have enclosed my résumé. From my 10 + years as a corporate facilities manager, I highlight below some relevant experience that matches your position criteria:

POSITION CRITERIA	RELEVANT EXPERIENCE
RENOVATION DESIGN EXPERIENCE	Over 10 + years' experience in 100 + interior renovation projects, which constituted over 90% of workload.
PROJECT MANAGEMENT	Managed all aspects of projects from inception through completion.
LEADERSHIP ABILITY	Several projects have been cited for trend-setting design excellence.
DESIGN-ENGINEERING CONSULTANTS	Evaluate, hire, and supervise over 15 consultants annually in present position.

PROJECT COST CONTROL — Developed unit price contracts, negotiated purchasing agreements/supply contracts, and exposed a double billing scheme, all of which have contributed to my reputation as a tough, but fair, manager who seeks *value.*

DESIGN CRITIQUE — Personally review all preliminary design proposals and all contract documents in present position. Phone centers and operator facilities have been cited by AT&T nationally for design excellence.

PROJECT COORDINATION/LIAISON — Coordinate with corporate user groups, upper management, landlords, vendors, contractors, and other diverse groups in current role of satisfying user group requirements while maintaining company standards/budgets on all projects.

As a frequent traveler and a member of your *Gold Passport* program, I am very familiar with the design standards of your hotels and identify strongly with the quality, trend-setting image of Hyatt projects. My current salary is in the mid forties.

In this ad response format you do all the work for the reader by carefully matching your requirements to his needs. If there were any category where experience didn't match perfectly, a statement of interest in this area or a plan for educational enhancement or general knowledge could be included. For example, "leadership" can be interpreted in any number of ways. It might mean "trend-setting design excellence"—as this writer interpreted it. Or it might mean leadership in terms of supervising and managing others. Either would be an acceptable response to the ad.

To Follow Up Research About a Specific Company or Organization

Suppose you've always wanted to work for a certain company and you have some clear ideas about what contributions you could make to that organization. You dig deep into your personal network and can't come up with any contacts into your dream company. A carefully conceived letter to the person two levels above the position you are targeting might open a door for you.

Sharon, a manager of corporate communications, decided to develop some consulting work during her job search transition. (She wanted to bring in extra money, and she felt it would help boost her self-confidence.) She could write extremely well, and *did* have a dream company that she wanted to work for. She identified the name of the director of creative and planning services at this company and sent him the following letter:

Dear Jack:

If you should ever need someone whose goal is to be one of the best writers in town on business, training, and technical issues, please call me so we can talk about it.

My specialty is translating technical or specialized information into easily understood language for end users who may not be familiar with the content. Thirteen years of experience have taught me how to learn new contents and/or new products and their technologies both quickly and efficiently. And as one who has learned to weather the anxieties inherent in any creative effort, I understand the mental process one must go through to organize and develop a mass of material into a disciplined, self-contained product.

I will let the enclosed speak for itself and only say further that as a member of the Society for Technical Communication, I agree wholeheartedly with its Code for Communicators, which reads in part:

I value the worth of the ideas I am communicating and the cost of developing and transmitting those ideas. I also value the time and effort spent by those who read or see or hear my communication.

I therefore recognize my responsibility to communicate technical information truthfully, clearly, and economically.

Sincerely,
Sharon Gold

Sharon included a couple of samples of her work and was planning to follow up in a few days with a telephone call to this individual and a request for a meeting. Believe it or not, she received a telephone call from someone to whom her letter had been forwarded and who had the authority to hire her. Sharon signed a consulting contract and established a very positive working relationship with the company. The relationship was so positive, in fact, that the company eventually offered her a full-time job, which she declined, preferring to remain on an external contractual basis.

To Follow Up a Meeting or Telephone Conversation

You have a wonderful (or not so wonderful) exploratory meeting or job interview. A follow-up letter will continue your marketing efforts and allow you to add some thoughts or ideas to what was discussed. Even a job interview calls for a follow-up letter to reflect your seriousness and professionalism.

A letter can accomplish a great deal that an interview cannot accomplish. An interview is almost always all verbal, and not everyone learns or concentrates best by listening. Some people have a more visual learning style, and providing them with written feedback and reaction can serve as protection against all your good points being forgotten.

To Contact a Search Firm

Think about who you know who works in a search firm. Have you helped recruiters fill jobs by referring them to possible candidates for jobs they described to you? Have you been contacted by search firms and saved the name and company for future reference? What search firms does your company use? (Go ask the human resources manager or the president if you don't know.) Which ones specialize in your industry or expertise? Which ones advertise in your industry journals? What search professionals could people in your network hook you into?

Search firms often have access to positions that are not advertised otherwise. It's important to note that search firms and employment (contingency) agencies are very different.

Search firms (otherwise known as headhunters or executive recruiters)—They operate on retainer, paid by the company hiring them to fill a position. Their fee is often up to 35 percent of the annual compensation of the position being filled. They are exclusively responsible for the position and are not competing with other agencies. Any person considered for the position they are handling must be funneled through the search firm.

Employment (contingency) agencies—They do not have an exclusive on filling a particular position. They may be competing with other agencies to provide the best candidate. Fees, also employer paid, can still be up to 35 percent of the annual compensation of the position being filled, but they are paid contingent upon a placement being made.

You can either give them a call (if you have a contact) or write them a letter and enclose a résumé. Many search firms will store your résumé in their computer if it looks like you have qualifications for the type and level of position they handle.

Recruiters do not read long letters accompanying résumés. They just want an overview of the type of position you are targeting, a statement of your accomplishments, and an honest statement of your current compensation package. It is best to give them the compensation, though we advise omitting discussion of salary in writing in most other instances.

The following letter, written by the same talented architect who wrote the want-ad response earlier in this section, was sent to a firm specializing in recruiting architects. It provides a good example of how to approach a search firm.

Dear Mr. Brink:

Do you have clients interested in an architect with solid corporate experience in interiors and facilities management? I believe my background would be attractive to the following clients:

- Consultants interested in enhancing design services to corporate clients and/or establishing new facilities management services for clients without "in-house" capabilities.
- Companies interested in upgrading or expanding "in-house" management functions or establishing functions presently nonexistent in the company.

My projects have been recognized for innovation and quality design. My experience and perspective from the role of "corporate client" offer exceptional potential for strengthening these services/functions to the right client.

I have enclosed my résumé for your review and consideration for any specific positions you may be handling in which my credentials would be a match. My geographical preferences are the Far West, Pacific Northwest, Southwest/Mountain regions or New England, but I would consider a challenging position in any location. My current salary is $52,300. Since I am single and enjoy world travel, I would be attracted to a position involving international travel.

Sincerely,
Timothy Pinder

In every case, Tim followed up the letter with a phone call and tried to generate further interest. Just a note here about how *not* to use search firms. If you are making a career change or if your credentials do not obviously make you qualified for the positions you are targeting, don't waste your time contacting search firms. If you want to change from the president of an office supply company to president of a manufacturing company, the search firm would probably not take a chance on you. Even though you might make a successful case for the fact that they both require the same skills, the search firm wants to present candidates with the exact qualifications requested by the hiring company. That is their job—to make good matches. They usually do not want to risk their reputation on a gut sense that someone would make a good candidate. That can only be done by the person doing the hiring.

In Response to an Article You Have Read

If you follow the local news in all local publications, you are likely to run across an article that stimulates your thinking, that gives you some ideas of what you could do for a particular company. Write a letter to the person who is the subject of the article, and include any of the following in your discussion:

- Discuss how you identify with him or her, or how your experience parallels that of the company, or how your unique perspective has helped you solve similar problems.
- Discuss what kind of contributions you could make to an organization like theirs.
- State how your experience in a different industry—or as an attorney, or a CPA—could lend an important new perspective to the problems with which they are dealing.
- Discuss predictions about the industry that you personally have which might be different from what the article reflects.
- Discuss ideas you have which might solve a problem that is described in the article.

People like to be singled out, to be complimented on what has been written about them—to be acknowledged. You can do this with honest reactions to what you have read, and possibly propel that written response into a face-to-face meeting.

To Accompany a Large Mailing

Significant disagreement surrounds the subject of sending large mailings. Many outplacement firms vehemently disapprove of large mailings, citing minute response rate as their reason. No one seems to disagree on support of limited, carefully researched mailings, but the question of whether large mailings are advisable remains controversial.

In John Lucht's *Rites of Passage at $100,000+* (Viceroy Press, 1988), "the insider's guide to absolutely everything about executive job-changing," the author presents a strong case for considering large, carefully researched mass mailings. As a matter of fact, he suggests sending out a thousand letters and résumés at the start of a job search. He appeals to the job searcher to "use direct mail to reach the whole universe of potential buyers." A 1 percent response rate, which is typical of direct-mail campaigns, would generate ten calls, from which an offer could evolve.

Naturally, who the thousand mailings are sent to would be crucial, and your research would be cut out for you. You'd want to make sure the names and companies were current and that you were sending to someone in your functional area who would be two levels above you. (Don't assume directories are current; check each name before you mail.)

If you decide to tackle such a mailing—which might be more

appropriate if you are doing a national search rather than a local one—Lucht recommends a letter format (which we have found effective), accompanied by a traditional chronological résumé. You are going for a match—your background with their needs.

The letter format that Lucht suggests can also be used for more limited mailings, or even in response to one company that you are targeting. He suggests beginning with a question that reflects your background, expertise, or interests. It might be:

- Could I help as a director of distribution or materials management?
- Have you considered expanding your product line to compete more effectively with the Japanese imports?
- Could you benefit from the expertise of a telecommunications specialist with broad-based experience in your industry?
- Are you looking for an educator with knowledge of cutting-edge developments about the brain and learning styles to impact your in-house training and education programs—and create some new ones?
- Do you need someone with turnaround experience to assist you in doing the downsizing that has been inevitable in our industry?

The next couple of paragraphs support your question by providing information about you, your expertise, your unique skills and talents, which will further pique his interest.

In Response to Meeting Someone

Let's say that in the course of your job search you decide to take a seminar or go hear a lecture. You're impressed with the presentation, which has a profound impact on the way you think. How could you turn this experience into a one-on-one interaction with the presenter? You could go up and speak to her following the presentation, though many others will probably be standing around competing for a few moments of her time as well. You could telephone her following the presentation and request a meeting. Or you could send a very personalized letter and follow that up with a telephone call and a request for a meeting.

Proposals

While you are deep into the job-search process and are uncovering possible job alternatives for yourself, you might begin thinking about how to translate your thoughts into an actual proposal. Many of you are used to writing proposals. As a management information systems professional, you may have had to write a proposal to justify purchase of a new computer system. As senior project plant engineer, you may have had to write a proposal to get funds allocated to modify the equipment to accommodate development of alternate products. As director of training, you may have had to write a proposal to get permission to design a new course on ethics.

Think about the proposals that have been made to you, requesting allocation of funds, permission to hire at a different level, or support for employee training on the computer. Perhaps as benefits administrator, you read proposals from benefits consulting firms, or as wage and salary specialist, you received proposals from firms competing to help you put in a new system to rate job positions.

If you have ever been a consultant who has charged a fee for your work, you've probably composed some form of proposal in order to get the job. It might have been sketchy, if the company knew you well and you didn't have to prove your competence. Nevertheless, you probably did submit something in writing.

It's that "something in writing" that we'd like to discuss here. Proposals can sometimes get your job search in motion again when it looks like things might be stalemated. You've gotten terrific response to your ideas. The company is seriously considering hiring you to expand their consulting arm. But it is a smaller, entrepreneurial computer systems consulting firm, and they are understandably hesitant about creating another $50,000-per-year job. You want to bring these negotiations to a head, get an offer, and get started.

You might consider developing a proposal. Describe what you would do, how, why, what it would cost them, how it would benefit them in the short and long term. Propose a lunch to discuss your proposal. In black and white it begins to seem real, and it might just get your future employer "off the dime."

Jake was experienced in starting up and running not-for-profit foundations, and in the course of his job search he uncovered an interesting opportunity with a fledgling local office. The politics of the situation were inhibiting the speed with which the decision to bring him on was being made. So he submitted a consulting contract covering an adequate time period to accomplish initial goals—with the hope that the contract would eventually lead to a full-time position, which it did.

Other examples of proposals that worked include Norm, a high-level customer service manager who wanted to be seriously considered for a position as an outplacement counselor and seminar leader in a start-up outplacement company. He clearly did not have the "formal" credentials necessary for the job. He wrote a proposal based on his ideas on how he would enhance what was already in place. He got the job.

And there was Janet, a marketing manager who was targeting a position as marketing director of a local hospital. She had a number of ideas of how to improve and expand the depth of the marketing already in place. She also had extensive knowledge of advertising throughout the hospital industry and decided to develop a comparative analysis of various hospitals' methods of advertising and their effectiveness. One day of work on a proposal led to her becoming a finalist for the position.

Finally there was a senior marketing manager interested in the arena of higher education who was being seriously considered for a newly created position as director of strategic planning. He was a hair's breadth away from an offer. To stimulate it, he developed a proposal for how the strategic planning process would unfold—including short- and long-term plans. The proposal was quite comprehensive and incorporated the knowledge he had acquired through researching his contact network for experts in this area. He received significant assistance from consultants who specialized in strategic planning in the higher-education market.

As you proceed through your job search, and as you are able to get potential employers to discuss problems or unmet needs, think about how to incorporate your ideas into a proposal format. It can even be an outline form. With it, you can request another lunch meeting, talk some more, and perhaps move the process another step toward employment.

The Third Dimension—
Your Portfolio

In some ways, a letter can be considerably more liberating than a résumé. You feel like yourself, you are not obligated to do a complete summary of your past work experience. It can reflect your energy and commitment, communicate integrity and initiative, and can help the reader project you into the organization's future, into a possible role in the company. A proposal is even more liberating, in that it contains exclusively your thinking, your ideas—a reflection of your unique beliefs and commitments.

Another way for you to become three-dimensional, to fight back against the sterility of the black-and-white pieces of thin paper that represent you, is to build a portfolio to show others. If you think that a portfolio is only for artists or graphic designers, you are right in one sense. They are the only ones expected to have portfolios. Unless they are extremely well known for their talent, they cannot get jobs without their portfolio.

Portfolios can be effective for you, too. You can pull together materials that reflect your background and experience. Have you ever been on the hiring end of selecting an ad agency or free-lance graphic artists? Remember how they "walked" you through their portfolio? You were interested in how they handled different assignments, on whether their work was consistently of high quality, on how creative they were.

Your present situation is comparable to that of choosing an ad agency—only in this case you are on the other end of the negotiation. Just as a graphic designer would not expect to be hired after showing one drawing, you should understand if you are not hired after a future employer surveys one or two pieces of paper—your résumé.

Consider a leather notebook, containing a number of different documents that reflect your experience and expertise, carefully encased in plastic or mounted attractively. This portfolio could be the point of discussion for a face-to-face meeting with a potential employer. You may be asked to leave it behind so that he can study it or show it to others.

A maintenance and facilities engineer, in addition to developing both a functional and chronological résumé, pulled together a rather impressive compilation of his previous project reports, evaluations of problems and subsequent bids, budget analyses and reports, memos sent to various groups in the company, training programs he had participated in developing, etc. He had helped develop a technical training program in conjunction with a technical school in the area and included letters of commendation both from the school and from participants in his program.

An attorney included several briefs she had prepared in her portfolio. A sales manager had recently brought with him a leather-bound copy of his dissertation to all his important interviews. He had also developed a paper that explained the evolution of his dissertation and what impact it had on his job.

A director of planning and institutional research for a local college was interested in transferring his skills to the private sector. He included in his portfolio a paper in which he described how he had been "building organizations" throughout his career, how corporate planning and development was a logical extension of his experience in both universities and government.

A public affairs director for a large public company became extremely enthusiastic about creating his portfolio. Over the past several years he had been involved in planning high-level national and international conferences and could include copy that demonstrated the evolution of his ideas for the conferences, as well as the conference programs themselves and follow-up evaluation sheets. He was also involved in setting up trade shows and included photographs of layout projections, as well as photographs of the trade shows in progress. As he began to think further about how to represent himself in his portfolio, he remembered that he had developed highly sophisticated computer tracking systems that could be included in the portfolio. Through this portfolio, he was able to project the bottom-line image that made him more marketable.

When thinking about what to include in your portfolio, consider the following:

- Reports, proposals, summaries, training programs, outlines, analyses, marketing plans, designs.
- Materials developed: films, videos, cassettes, manuals, guidelines.
- Articles written (whether published or not), contributions to newsletters or in-house magazines; articles about you in industry newsletters or publications.
- Letters written to you by former bosses, colleagues, or people who reported to you; letters of congratulation.
- Create anything that might add a dimension to the portfolio: a summary of programs you developed; a description of negotiations that led to pulling a company out of chapter 11; and so forth.

You'll want to pick and choose carefully. Include enough material to reflect some of your unique talents and experiences, but not too much to become cumbersome or repetitive. Obviously you'll want to be careful not to include anything proprietary or confidential.

So get busy collecting materials for your portfolio. Rummage through your old papers and reports. Reread any proposals you wrote and letters of commendation you received. Cut out articles either about you or that quoted you. And begin to put your portfolio together.

So there you have it. We've suggested many ways for you to increase your repertoire of written marketing tools to be used during your search. We hope you are game to try them—to write one or more résumés, to send letters whenever appropriate, to create proposals to carry a possibility to completion, and to put together a portfolio. It may seem like a lot of work to you, and it is. But the doors you might open using written communication could far surpass what would be possible without it.

5

The Data Dimension
Where to Look for Information for Your Job Search

We would like to convince you to put visits to the library on your weekly agenda. We'd also like to encourage you to become tuned into the information at your fingertips: news programming on television, newspapers and magazines, local lectures and seminars, association meetings, panel discussions—all can provide you with valuable information for potential targets for your job search. But in order to get you to raise your antennae, and to actually get you into the library on a regular basis throughout your job search, we knew we'd need to give you some examples of success stories in which uncovered information led to successful job searching. Following are some examples of the positive impact that such research had on clients' job searches:

- A manufacturing manager read about a small, privately held chemical company that was proud of its achievement, but was suffering growing pains due to new government regulations. He wrote a letter to the president, shared his own successful experience in dealing with a similar situation, and was invited in for a meeting.

- In a specialized newsletter for leasing companies, a controller read about the difficulty that leasing companies were having in an area that related to his expertise. He composed a letter to illustrate how he could address this problem, and sent out twenty-five letters and résumés. He received twelve telephone calls in response, an absolutely unheard of response in comparison to direct mail's usual 1 to 2 percent success rate.

- A supervisor of reservationists at an airline researched the banking industry—read everything she could get her hands on—familiarized herself with the current state of affairs of the industry in her city, and targeted training positions with this extensive knowledge base. She landed a job as a trainer in a bank.

- An MIS expert read of the difficulty technological changes were causing at an insurance company. He networked into the company and eventually was hired as director of new technology, a newly created position to deal with this problem.

- A social worker with experience in management wanted to relocate to Oregon. He researched all companies in Oregon with in-house employee assistance programs, as well as all agencies dealing with family problems. He targeted the companies, sent letters, went to Oregon to do a job search, and landed a job as executive director of an agency specializing in family problems.

- A manager from a coal company accessed a data base to uncover all companies in the energy field in the geographical locations he was targeting. With the current list he did a mailing that led to some interviews.

What will you find with your antennae up—alertly scanning libraries, book stores, newspapers, journals, and television programs or taking in lectures and association meetings? You'll find that you can pick up the speed of your search by building on your knowledge base. Your creative juices will start churning, and your ideas will stimulate your thinking about companies and individuals to target. Having read a book or an article on a relevant subject can trigger a terrific conversation. Having researched a subject could put you in a position where you have information that could prove valuable to others. They'll *want* to talk with you.

Where to Research

When we say "research" we hope you don't cringe. If you widen your focus to include information from some of the following sources, you'll find yourself learning, challenged—and above all, you'll become a lot more interesting to others.

1. *Libraries*—including public, academic, community college (for information about trades), corporate libraries, and interlibrary loan (to gain access to the holdings outside of the library you are in). Anybody can use most public and university libraries—though you cannot always check out books or references. Corporate libraries can be accessed through your network; tap someone who works at a corporation whose library has information you want.

2. *Library research firms*—to uncover difficult-to-find information on privately held companies that you are investigating. Found in most major cities, several are national in scope. Two of the better-known information brokers are FIND/SVP in New York City and Washington Researchers in Washington, D.C.

3. *Bookstores*—to see what's new on the shelf, especially in the section relevant to your target. Check bookstores with unusual collections of magazines. If you want to target industry with an idea for school partnership, get a copy of Naisbitt's and Aburdene's *Re-inventing the Corporation* so

Don't tell me — he's conducting a job search!

that you can discuss their cutting-edge ideas—and even give examples of what is working in Texas.

4. *The public relations office of corporations and organizations* (also known as community relations, press, or public information offices)—to learn about various corporations and their subsidiaries. Public companies make their annual reports available to the public, and privately held companies often have brochures available.

5. *Business information services*—to check their current awareness publications, which are updated continuously, focus on a narrow topic or industry, are distributed to a limited audience, and accept no advertising. Three major types of publications meet these criteria: newsletters, loose-leaf services, and syndicated intelligence services. Some of the leading names in the production of market intelligence reports are: A. C. Nielson Company, Audits & Surveys, Inc., and the Market Research Corporation of America.

6. *Computer data bases*—to generate lists of people for direct-mail targeting letters. These data bases are generally available through libraries and private data base companies (check the yellow pages), and increasingly available (though very expensive, unless you are skilled at accessing them) to people who have personal computers, modems, and are hooked up to an on-line service. One of the largest providers is DIALOG Information Services, a subsidiary of the Lockheed Corporation, offering over two hundred data bases, two-thirds of which have direct business application. Whatever service you use, chances are good that the information is current.

7. *Trade associations and other nonprofit organizations* (including university research centers)—for specialized information in a particular field. These organizations can be identified through special directories available through most libraries. They often have newsletters or other publications.

8. *Newspaper morgues*—for articles relevant to your search. Some are still in operation, but only a few will let outsiders gain access to their clippings. You can, however, access newspaper articles at a good public library that cross-references and stores this information. If you know the issue of an article, they'll often send you a copy at no charge.

9. *Federal and state government offices, as well as the Small Business Administration*—to explore government jobs or for information on starting a small business or evaluating a business you are thinking of buying.

10. *Chambers of commerce locally and worldwide*—to uncover names of individuals in localities and to find out about a particular city or region.

11. *Bankers, stockbrokers, financial institutions*—to get financial information, including annual reports and 10K's, that could be useful.

12. *Radio and TV stations*—for programs relating to your field. Stations will often provide the transcript of a program that could lead to information or people to contact.

13. *College alumni offices*—for lists of alumni, which can be useful, especially if you are a graduate of the same college. Often there are placement directors who may be helpful.
14. *College professors*—to find out about trends in a field of interest. When professors go to conferences each year, they meet colleagues in other parts of the country or hear about information through position papers. Reconnect with professors whose classes you have attended or seek out academicians in fields relevant to yours.
15. *Newspapers* (local and out of town)—to scan for the untold riches to be found within. For instance, some cities publish upcoming business or professional meetings every week. If you know what day of the week this information is published, you can keep track of organizations pertinent to a particular field and attend a meeting. You might uncover associations that have placement services, such as the local chapter of ASTD (American Society of Training and Development) or the IABC (International Association of Business Communicators) or the Planning Forum (a strategic planning group by invitation only—no problem, just find a way to get invited!). If you join some of these associations, you may have access to job descriptions that they receive.
16. *Comprehensive business directories* for a particular city for current business information. In St. Louis, Missouri, for example, a directory called *Sorkin's* lists most businesses in that city and includes data such as names of officers, number of employees, annual revenue, when it was founded, and a description of the business. Equivalent directories can be found in other major cities, often through the chamber of commerce.
17. *Executive recruiters or search firms*—to brainstorm with them. Headhunters know a lot about what is going on. They can even lead you to colleagues in other fields.
18. *Résumé banks*—to list your résumé. For a modest fee these computerized services will enter your résumé among others for corporations to graze through. (Be careful to choose one that is legitimate.)

Reframing About Research

You might think that a list of reference books that have been useful in some job searches might be all that you need. But we know from experience in working with others like you that simply pointing you in the right direction is not enough. We need to *convince* you about the need to use these materials, help you overcome your prejudice against using the library or other repositories of information—as well as show you how to use them.

No one asks to be fired or goes out of their way to invite the experience, but after the fact—after landing a new job and settling into a comfortable life-style—those who have been fired often state that they are grateful for the experience. They speak of the new horizons that were opened to them as a result. Likewise with research, which can begin a habit of lifelong learning and enable you to permanently expand your horizons.

Resourcing—A Mother Lode of Information

Did you know that the word *resourcing* is used both for looking for information in libraries as well as a mining term in the search for lead, zinc, silver, and gold? In mining, resources are "reserves" or hypothetical and speculative deposits that have not yet been discovered. In fact, many productive mines have been found by accident. For example, the famed lead, zinc, and silver district of the Coeur d'Alenes in Idaho was discovered when a prospector chasing his burro saw the fresh minerals exposed in a boulder, broken by the fleeing animal.

Using the metaphor of mining for looking for information in your job search may enable you to understand the usefulness of the search, whether the kernels are found accidentally or purposefully. And while some miners never strike it "rich," we can assure you that if you put at least as much effort into using the library and other related areas as most people put into researching a European vacation, you will be sure to find information that will give your dreams direction.

If Alvin Toffler, author of *The Third Wave* (Morrow, 1980), and others like him are right, information and technology are the commodities of the new age we are entering. The library today is a place where information and technology come together to provide the user with access to the entire planet. If the factory was key to the industrial age, then the library might well be key to the information/technology age.

Yet most people are prevented from using the library effectively for a number of reasons, most of which date back to experiences in high school or college. Remember the librarian who wore a permanent scowl and seemed totally inaccessible, always preoccupied with shelving books rather than being available to help you? Well, today's reference librarians are not necessarily a clone of the ones you grew up with. They may have been born about 1960, are comfortable with emerging technology, and are eager to teach and help you.

If you have properly identified a true reference librarian, as opposed to a clerk whose job is to simply shelve and catalogue books, you should realize that times have definitely changed. Here is a person to add to your list of allies. He or she can help you to understand the layout of the library, show you how to use it, and connect you with specialized librarians in corporate libraries who may offer you use of the library as a professional courtesy.

If you engage the librarians, treat them like a true ally in your search, you may find that, like us, you will actually receive messages on your answering machine about a new reference that you might find helpful. Newspapers and periodicals, abstracts, microform, film, video, CD-ROM (Compact Disc—Read Only Memory)—there is a world of information awaiting you.

The library is the place to accidentally stumble on something that might serendipitously lead you into a new job target. Maybe it's a new field that you found thumbing through the *Guide to Business Periodical Literature*. Maybe it's a reference you found in *Gale's*

Directory of Publications or the *Encyclopedia of Associations*. Before you saw Elizabeth Fowler's "Careers" column in the *New York Times* (published every Tuesday), you might not have known that there was a field of ethics management or issues management. Now a whole new world is opening up to you, including the names that were mentioned in the articles as potential individuals to write to for further information.

You might now be interested in thoroughly researching this field you stumbled upon, asking your friendly reference librarian for further clues about where you could find some in-depth information. Time well spent in the front end of a job search researching a field can provide you with information and targets that will be invaluable later on.

Let's say you are exploring the transition from advertising to public relations. You know something about the field from your own experience, but you're open to expanding that knowledge. You will undoubtedly come across the Public Relations Society of America (PRSA), the association that you discovered in *The Encyclopedia of Associations*. Your librarian led you to *O'Dwyer's Directory of Public Relations Executives, O'Dwyer's Directory of Public Relations Firms,* or the *Standard Directory of Advertisers and Advertising Agencies,* and you now are able to carefully target the professionals in your city or geographical target.

While you may be aware that the library provides access to job listings through *The Wall Street Journal's Job Listings* and the Help Wanted sections of numerous out-of-town newspapers, you may not have remembered to look at trade or professional journals such as *Advertising Age* or *Personnel Journal* to find job listings in the field of advertising or personnel. Almost every field from acupuncture to zoology has at least one trade journal, and many of these publications list openings as they occur. Knowing how to access these trade journals might further extend your opportunities. Recruiters who specialize in certain industries often display ads or articles in these publications.

Another conventional use of the library in a job search is to use its resources to prepare for an upcoming interview. Annual reports will provide you with information about the company's bottom line and mission, information you'll need to conduct an intelligent interview. Many libraries keep annual reports on the major corporations in that city in current files, available for you to photocopy.

You might not have thought about using a library to help you find statistics and other useful data to substantiate a proposal you might want to write to meet an organization's unmet needs, to create your own job, or to demonstrate your capabilities once inside the company. As you know from our discussion of marketing techniques, proposals—unlike résumés, which look to past accomplishments—provide a potential employer with evidence of your ability to be proactive. The library can help you uncover information you need.

Another less-than-obvious use of the library is to research an article that you might write for a professional or trade journal yourself. "Nonoperational time" (see chapter 1) provides you with an opportunity to toot your own horn and become visible through your own contribution to the field. Other job searchers who have done this have been surprised with the phone calls and letters they have received from colleagues and potential employers. They were able to overcome the familiar feeling of being "one down" in a job-search situation. They were also amazed at how much respect people in print are given in our culture.

If you get used to going to the library, it is a good place to go in between meetings. With the librarians as your allies and increasing knowledge on how to use it well, you will find it a friendly place that invites you in to discover its wonders. Have we lured you in yet? Let's discuss specifically what to look for once you get there.

How to Use the
Library Effectively

Whether you are using the New York Public Library or a public library in Duluth, Minnesota, there are common features about gaining access to the library and using it effectively. Reference sources can essentially be found in four different places within the library walls.

First, and probably most familiar to you, is the card catalogue, which lists all the holdings in the library. Most libraries are now computerized, but if your library hasn't yet converted to a computerized system, you may find the familiar series of small cabinets that contain index cards with information about the sources available to the patrons. Using this manual system to locate material may be cumbersome and slow, though it can permit you to stumble on information more easily than an automated system does.

Chances are that your library has converted or is in the process of converting to a computerized catalogue system, known as a "library automation system." It won't take you long to get comfortable with locating information in this computerized system; just allow yourself an extra half hour to get comfortable. And don't hesitate to ask for help if you need it.

A librarian would be able to tell you whether his library had COMCATs (Computer Output Microfilm Catalogs) so that you could see holdings of other branches. He could also assist you in accessing other libraries' holdings throughout the country through a joint computer cataloguing system called OCLC (On-line Computer Library Center, Inc.).

A reference librarian could assist you in looking in the card catalogue for listings of specialized directories and encyclopedias that will be helpful to you, such as *The Standard Periodical Directory, Ulrich's International Periodicals Directory, The National Directory of Newsletters and Reporting Services,* and *The Encyclopedia of Associations,* to name a few. This same librarian could give you a tour of the areas in which sources like these are kept or point out books that might be particularly helpful to you, such as *Business Information: How to Find It, How to Use It* by Michael R. Lavin (Ory Press, 1987).

Your librarian might also lead you to special in-house files that the library has been keeping over the years that would help you. For instance, a reference librarian at a university library told us that she was working with library interns to develop a body of information about local businesses from newspaper clippings. This information could be invaluable because it would include details about corporations and organizations in the area that could be found no other way. If your library has such rich local files, imagine the help it could be to you in your job search.

If you are the type who likes to survey the territory first, you would find David Beasley's *How to Use a Research Library* (Oxford University Press, 1988) helpful. Or better yet, read *Knowing Where to Look: The Ultimate Guide to Research* by Lois Horowitz (Writer's Digest Books, 1988), the book we have found to be most helpful. One of our favorite reference librarians actually telephoned us to tell us to come in and get this book!

Next, after the computerized card-catalogue system, look in the indexes and abstracts that identify periodical literature, including magazines, business journals, trade journals, and newspapers such as the *New York Times, Wall Street Journal,* and *Christian Science Monitor.*

While you will find listings of these periodicals in magazine-length and book-bound form, they can also be found increasingly in automated form in most libraries. The CD-ROM, for example, is a small disc that looks like an audio CD and holds the equivalent of five hundred books or 250,000 pages of information. The CD-ROM system looks and works much like the computer that you might have used to browse through the card catalogue. Yet the optical technology will allow you to scan thousands of pages of periodical information with the push of a button, and you can print out a listing of any articles that might be of interest to you. Whether you access the periodical literature manually or using computerized equipment, you'll be locating information that you can follow up on in the magazines and newspapers found in the library.

For instance, let's say that you have worked in human resources and are considering a move into the field of outplacement. (Actually, many top-notch outplacement counselors were formerly human resource professionals.) You could go to the *Guide to Periodical Business Literature* or a CD-ROM equivalent to access titles to all the articles on outplacement. Then judging from the titles listed and depending on what magazines are available at the library, you could select a number of articles to read (you can always order them through interlibrary loan if you don't mind waiting). You might go to the index for the *New York Times* or the *Wall Street Journal* as well, to review the articles written about outplacement in those newspapers in the last several months.

Again, thumbing through a manual system rather than using a computer would allow you to stumble on an article listed in *The New York Times Index* about a woman who is a humor consultant to corporations. You might want to follow up by reviewing the article about her on microfilm, the method in which most newspapers are stored in libraries today. This might provide you with credible support for your proposal to companies for ways to incorporate humor into their training programs.

A third area to look at in the library would be the government documents section. Some libraries are depositories for federal or state government publications. You will be amazed at the breadth and scope of the information available through the various government agencies. If your library is not a depository, your reference librarian could more than likely help you understand how to gain access to government publications and how they might be useful to you in your particular search.

The major tool for identifying government publications is the "Monthly Catalog," issued by the superintendent of documents, also issued on CD-ROM. Another reference is "GPO Sales Publications Reference File" (PRF), published as well by the superintendent of documents (on microfiche only).

Finally, the fastest but most expensive way to gain information is through data base searching, available at many university libraries for a fee, as well as through private companies. If you have been provided with outplacement support, you can request data base searches; often their cost will be included in your program. Data bases are enormous amounts of information stored in computers, organized in numerous different ways, referenced and cross-referenced for easy access, and updated regularly. Accessing data bases efficiently takes some training, and the professional helping you can help you ask the appropriate questions to uncover the data you need.

Librarians have described data base searching as the Cadillac of their services. Because of the expense, often eighty to ninety dollars per hour, librarians suggest that you exhaust print sources before using on-line data base searching. Accessing information in this way can be useful to locate obscure information, to narrow information down, to generate lists of individuals to target in various industries or parts of the country, or to get at activities and news that is just happening or breaking now. It is also useful for melding two concepts.

For instance, a person who is interested in exploring companies where there is an emphasis on both safety and corporate wellness could do an on-line data base search to uncover this information. Or an on-line data base search could be conducted to identify where the top corporate wellness centers are located. You could then target the companies that you have uncovered.

A Sample Library
Data Search

We would like to use as an example the library search of a former client to demonstrate how research can be used effectively in a job search.

Janet had been an outstanding, successful marketing manager for computer systems with a major corporation, responsible for revenues of $8 million to $10 million annually. Another area of her expertise was in developing and managing cutting-edge training programs for new sales recruits, as well as continuing training for experienced sales representatives. Since many of the major accounts she supervised were in the financial sector, Janet became interested in targeting a senior marketing position in a financial institution. She had also become interested in the newly evolving concept of marketing director for a major law firm, ever since she had read an article stating that 20 percent of the nation's larger law firms had hired senior-level marketing directors. Her final scenario was to work for a management consulting firm specializing in marketing or training of trainers.

Following the procedure of an organized library search laid out by

Lois Horowitz in *Knowing Where to Look,* Janet dug up the following information that helped her get closer to her scenarios:

- *Periodical articles.* Looking in the *Business Periodicals Index,* Janet found several articles that were worth pursuing:
  - –Under "Bank Marketing" she found "Guidelines for Establishing the Marketing Function" in a publication entitled *Bank Marketing;* "A Real Nice Bank" in *American Demographics;* "The Role of Commercial Banks in a Securitized World" in *Bankers Magazine;* "Sports Marketing Can Add Points to Your Scoreboard" in *Bank Marketing;* and "Tennessee Bank's Campaign Theme Is Talk of Town" in *Bank Marketing.*
  - –Under "Employee Training" she found "Good Followers Are Worth Training" in *Nation's Business;* "Training and Education: The Competitive Edge" in *Personnel Administrator;* "Preparing Useful Performance Indicators" in *Training Development Journal;* "An Organized Approach to Staff Development" in *Accountancy;* "How HRD Can Contribute to Company Expansion" in *Agriculture;* and "Training Americans for Work: Industry's Monumental Challenge" in *Industry Week.*
  - –Under "Marketing Consultants" she found "A Guide to Companies Offering Sampling Services" in *AdWeek Marketing Week.*
  - –Under "Marketing" Janet found a list of alternative terms including "Advertising," "Marketing Strategy," "Product Differentiation," "Product Life Cycle," "Target Marketing," and "Women in Marketing"—suggested headings under which to look for more information. There were also useful articles under "Marketing Management" and "Marketing Strategy."
- *Encyclopedias.* In *The Encyclopedia of Associations* Janet found the following organizations that were worth pursuing:
  - –Bank Marketing Association, which has 4,500 members and puts out the following publications: *Bank Marketing*

Monthly, Marketing Update Monthly, Community Bank Marketing Newsletter, Trust Marketing Resource, and *Information Center Newsletter Quarterly.* She discovered that this organization has an annual convention with exhibits.

–Financial Marketing Association, which has 710 members and publishes *Marketing Exchange* and *Credit Union Marketing Magazine*

–National Association of Bank Women

* *References.* In *Directories in Print 1989* Janet found the following directories that were of interest to her in identifying key people in the industry that she was pursuing:

    –*Directory of Bank Marketing Services; Marketing Alumni Directory,* Proctor & Gamble; *Marketing and Sales Career Directory; Marketing Association of St. Louis— Membership Directory; Marketing Management,* "What Top Sales and Marketing Executives Earn" edition [executive compensation]; *Advertising Association—Membership Directory International; Advertising Sales Association— Directory of National Members and their Represented Newspapers in the United States and Canada;* and *Who's Who in Advertising*

    Who's Who Among Human Services Professionals; Training & Development Organizations Directory; and *Who's Who in Training and Development*

    In *The Standard Periodical Directory* Janet found the following avenues to pursue:

    –*Marketing Review; Consultant's News; Consultant Practice; Consultant's Newsletter; Consultation; Consulting Opportunities Journal;* and *Consulting Services*

Each of these sources told Janet very clearly how to retrieve the information that she was looking for. After going through the *Business Periodicals Index,* she identified which of the periodicals were on hand at her library. Articles in magazines that were not owned by her library could be ordered through interlibrary loan.

Janet was amazed at just how helpful these sources were to her because she had a clearer picture about what marketing managers were doing in banking, about marketing in law firms, and about the current state of consulting organizations. If she didn't want to relocate, these new contacts in other locations could surely give her insights and possible names of whom to contact locally.

Although she didn't locate a lot of information about the emerging field of law firm marketing, she did uncover the name of an organization of law firm marketers that had just recently formed, and one article about law firm marketers in her city. One phone call to someone named in the article led her effortlessly to several other articles, which were photocopied and mailed to her by this contact. If this strategy had not led her to adequate information, she was considering doing a data base search to uncover more about law firm marketing.

With the information Janet had uncovered, she became more self-confident about marketing herself into job targets which were not replicating her highly successful experience of marketing in the computer systems field. She no longer felt inadequate when making the initial telephone calls to explore the contributions she might make to banking or consulting. She knew enough about what was currently happening in each area to translate her background and experience into their future. She felt smart and current, and it showed in how well she marketed herself.

Using Words in Print
and the Media as Stimuli

While you were busy fulfilling the responsibilities of your job, you were no doubt regularly reading relevant materials such as trade journals, professional journals, newspapers, literature produced by research organizations about your industry, and perhaps the *Wall Street Journal*. Your reason for doing this reading was probably to keep abreast of the news relevant to your business or industry so that you could make intelligent decisions.

We suggest that you continue this reading, but now expand the purpose of your perusing these publications to collecting names of people to write to, industries to approach, needs that in your opinion are going unfilled.

Trade journals alone provide:

- Current information about the industry.
- Personnel changes in major companies.
- Announcements of new products or government contracts.
- Warnings of impending changes in government or other regulations.
- Details of trends in the industry.
- Present management techniques.

Here is much information that will be of use to you as you plot your course and plan your search. While you'll still be scanning the information as you once might have done, you'll now be reading with a different lens, looking for clues that could lead to job opportunities.

And you'll want to raise your antennae even further to publications outside your field and industry, as well as to all local and national publications that you find interesting. Additionally, television and radio news can give you good information about changes in companies locally and nationally; news of mergers and acquisitions or of improved earnings for the first time in six quarters can lead to new target possibilities.

Want ads in local papers, the *Wall Street Journal,* the *New York Times* and in trade and professional journals are important to read, too. Not just as sources of leads for jobs but for the information they can transmit to you about industries, hirings, changes in company structure, and most of all (we hate to say it), the jargon. If you are coming from the not-for-profit world to industry, for example, then getting familiar with industry's marketing jargon is essential. Becoming aware of words like "needs assessment," used often in the training field, is necessary if you are moving from teaching in a public school or university to training in the corporate sector. Reading the want ads can fill you in on how positions are described and on specific responsibilities accompanying varying job descriptions.

Scanning the want ads, you'll be reading between the lines to identify companies that may be looking for electrical engineers but might also need a turnaround manager or a systems analyst, even though they are not advertising for one. These ads can help you spot companies that you didn't even know existed, and then you can be creative about targeting them through use of your contact network.

You might consider ordering an out-of-town newspaper through your newsstand and read the job advertisements in the *Los Angeles Times* or the *Chronicle of Higher Education,* for instance. You could identify new job targets that you could market yourself into in your part of the country. Out-of-town yellow pages can provide you with a view of business and industry in a particular location. If you are targeting outplacement counseling positions and you find no outplacement firms listed, you could sell the idea of creating an outplacement division at a CPA or management consulting or search firm. The key is to use these publications more creatively than they are usually used—not just at face value but as a stimulus to creative options that might otherwise not occur to you.

Researching the Community— Where Have You Been Visible?

You may think that you know no one now that could help you out in your job search. But chances are excellent that you know more people and that more people know you than you are presently aware of. You may *think* that a certain individual would never remember you or that your contact was too long ago to permit you to connect with them. But more often than not, others do have a clear recollection of connecting with you and do remember that conversation at a trade association meeting or that interaction over the telephone about a local bank-sponsored luncheon featuring a prominent economist. If you remember the interaction, chances are that they will, too.

It is fairly typical for outplacement counselors to tell initial job searchers to make a list all of their contacts, people that could be called during their job search. The only problem is that many people have a great deal of trouble making the list—and have *very* creative reasons why they should exclude certain persons or groups of persons from their list.

In order to approach creating a list of people to help you during your job search, we encourage you to stop censoring your list. Everyone who comes to mind is *written down*. You can always omit names later.

Now in order to generate this list of helpful people, it might be helpful for you to focus first on *where you have been*. That is, where have you come in contact with other people and what interactions have resulted? The following questions should assist you in your quest to remember who you know and who knows you:

1. Think about your interactions at your previous jobs, when other people had the opportunity to work with you, see you in action demonstrating your capabilities. Who were these people?

2. In the line of duty, as part of your job, in what situations have you found yourself in contact with individuals from other companies? With whom were you in contact at luncheons sponsored by vendors or local associations?

3. Think about any vendors or clients with whom you have had contact, and the situations in which you have interfaced with them. Who were they, and what networks do they have that you personally may not have?

4. In what situations have you been involved in religiously affiliated activities? Who has had the opportunity to work with you or hear you speak?

5. What about your investment decisions in your personal life? Do you have a working relationship with any stockbrokers, financial planners, CPAs, attorneys, insurance brokers, real estate agents? Under what circumstances do you know these people and do they know you?

6. What trade associations have had breakfast or luncheon or evening meetings that you have attended? Who spoke that impressed you? Did you speak to them afterward? Were you involved in the planning? Did you have any particularly stimulating conversations that you could refer to when calling someone?

7. What groups have you spoken to as a guest speaker? Who did you meet before and after the talk? Who called to thank you for your contribution?

8. Have you ever been interviewed? If so, who interviewed you and for what publication? Are there people who called to congratulate you?

9. What conferences have you attended either locally or nationally? Who do you know from those extended meetings who may be good persons to contact? Do those people interface with any groups that you may be interested in connecting with? Do the conferences represent associations that have placement services? Who could you contact?

10. Are you involved with your children as a sports leader, in any special clubs, in a neighborhood association? Who has seen you in action or knows a bit about you who might be a good contact?

11. Do you continue to be involved in any alumni association from high school, college, or graduate school? What people do you recall from these groups?

12. What about your spouse's activities and the associates he or she has become friendly with? Have you met them?

13. With whom have you had lunch over the past year? Look back through your calendar and remember where you went, what you talked about, with whom you talked.

14. Who have you met on out-of-town vacations who could be a possible contact?

15. If your children are currently or have been in college, what other parents have you met on such events as Parents' Weekend?

16. Where do your relatives work? Whom do they know? Go through your personal telephone directory or lists that you

may have compiled in sending out birth, confirmation, or wedding announcements and Christmas cards.

17. Don't forget your closest friends. They'll want to help you but just won't know how unless you clue them in.
18. Are you on any boards of directors or advisory boards that meet monthly or quarterly? Everyone on those boards is a possible target, and they have all seen you in action.

After you have applied your mental energy to remembering these people, you may then want to make a list in priority order of those you want to tap first for information about your career scenarios and job targets. You'll be amazed at how quickly you'll acquire useful information.

On Going to Seminars, Meetings, Conferences

A senior management-training specialist for a large corporation, with two master's degrees in the health-care field, has an interesting philosophy on how to do an effective job search. When anticipating the need to look for a job, she looks for seminars, workshops, or conferences that will be attended by people who have the level job to which she is aspiring. Not only will she then be exposed to subject matter that intrigues her, but she will have the beginnings of a contact network of people doing that job.

Even if in the past you seldom attended workshops or seminars or went to association meetings, now is a good time to think about exploring this method of both enlarging your perspective and getting in touch with job opportunities that are not visible to you in other ways.

One client, Len, formerly a sales manager for a beer distributor, decided to attend association meetings during his job-search period. He had just recently joined his trade association and consequently knew very few people there. He attended a total of nine or ten meetings in a two-month period, most of those being his own trade association's meetings. At one of these meetings he heard of a job opening in Denver—at a competitor of his previous company—a sales manager position that sounded like it was made for him. He learned of it from an executive of the company who happened to sit next to him at dinner and was discussing the company's needs.

Subsequently, Len accepted a position with this company with greater responsibility, territory, and financial remuneration than the position he had first heard about. Yet had he not interviewed for the sales manager position, he would not have heard about or been considered for the position of regional sales manager he eventually accepted. (The position was never advertised; just word of mouth was used to identify candidates.)

Here are some other examples of how attending seminars and meetings can lead to jobs:

- A design engineer attended a national convention for environmental engineers at her own expense two months following her termination. Through networking at the convention, distributing her résumé, and meeting with employers who were looking for employees, she received an offer for a position at her level.
- A marketing director attended a breakfast meeting of a local women's commerce association meeting. She introduced herself as a marketing director in search of a position and was approached after the meeting by a recruiter who was trying to fill a marketing job. She got the job.
- An administrator for a hospital who wanted to enter the field of training attended the local meetings of the National Association of Training and Development, became active on two committees, made friends, and in four months was called to interview for two different training positions.
- An attorney specializing in construction law participated on a panel with real estate and construction experts during his job transition. He got a list of all those attending and did carefully targeted telephoning a week after the panel discussion. Everyone he called was complimentary of his presentation and eager to help in his search.

You may have a special area of expertise that would qualify you to give a talk or be on a panel at an association meeting or dinner meeting of some organization. Speaking before a group is an excellent way to make contacts quickly and to present yourself as extremely capable and very marketable.

One final thought about attending meetings and conferences. Think about attending ones *outside* your field of expertise, outside your normal exposure. Cross-fertilizing with people in other areas will generate ideas, possibilities, and options for employment that you may not have thought of otherwise. If you are a controller, try attending a meeting of marketing professionals. If you are in purchasing, try attending a computer association meeting. You will learn of industries other than yours and learn of openings otherwise not advertised.

Take some time to think about what meetings you could attend that would truly interest you and might further your job search in unpredictable ways. Ask friends about associations they belong to and whether they can bring along a guest. Call the president or membership chairperson and tell them your interest in attending. Build this into your job-search campaign, and you will expand your contacts considerably.

Consider attending the annual or semiannual conventions for the associations in the fields you are considering that you have found listed in *The Encyclopedia of Associations*. If you are well informed about the nature of the convention through correspondence with the president or membership chairperson, you may be making a wise investment in your future by attending. Conventions that are national or international in scope will usually feature the highly visible and accomplished people in that field who are presenting cutting-edge information and developments. The subject of their presentation could very well stimulate you to think about new ways to target your job objectives and new ideas for proposals.

Are you convinced that research will help you conduct a better job search? Are you full of resolve to go to the library this week—and to resource the rich reserves in all your personal

Let's not bother him now, Marge. He's job searching!

contacts throughout the search? Doing so will be the best protection against regressing into a funk about being "unemployed" or allowing yourself to be distracted and spending valuable time fixing the roof or building a deck. Sure those things need to be done—but only on weekends. Getting accustomed to doing research, to expanding your horizons—to uncovering the information that will make you feel smart and definitely improve your presentation—will prevent you from being concerned when you hear unemployment statistics. And you'll learn so much through this process that you'll be energized and stimulated throughout your job-search transition.

6

The Dialogue Dimension
Communicating with Potential Employers and Others Throughout the Job Search

When Amy Edmondson was a freshman at Harvard, she took a course called synergetics, the science of spatial complexity, which excited and challenged her and stimulated her imagination. She followed up with other courses taught by the same professor, Arthur Loeb, and when she ran out of classes to take from Professor Loeb, she did an independent study on Buckminster Fuller's *Synergetics*. When she heard "Bucky" speak at MIT a year later, she found herself spellbound by what she describes as a "life-changing experience," firsthand exposure to Bucky's brilliance combined with his profound belief in the universe.

Amy had a second opportunity to hear Bucky speak—and continued to be thrilled by this great twentieth-century thinker. As luck would have it, Bucky was speaking at Harvard and was housed in her dorm with his wife, Anne Fuller. Amy was able to talk with him informally over several meals, though she remembers being very careful not to make a "nuisance" of herself. She again found herself deeply impressed, now by her dialogues with Bucky. Later that summer she heard that Bucky was going to speak on Nantucket Island in the Unitarian church, and she made a point of going to hear him. She just couldn't get enough of this man's expansive ideas and empowering vision of a world that worked for everyone—she had so much to learn from him.

Earlier in the day, prior to the evening lecture, Bucky happened to run into Amy on the street, and he asked her where he knew her from. Astonished that this eighty-five-year-old man who traveled and spoke extensively around the world, meeting thousands and thousands of people a year, would remember her, she told him they had met at Harvard. He then proceeded to mention specifically what their conversations had been about. (Obviously she had not made a "nuisance" of herself in those interactions!)

Amy wrote her thesis on one aspect of Buckminster Fuller's work, "tensegrity" structures, and began thinking about her first job after graduation. She was graduating early and had a strong desire to apply what she had learned and to make a contribution— but very little idea of where she could work or what exactly she could do with her education. She visited the career planning office but afterward still felt vague about what she could do with her degree in engineering and applied sciences and visual and environmental studies. Then she got a flash—why not write Bucky himself and ask if he knew of any organizations where she might work? Though she felt presumptuous writing the letter, she figured she had very little to lose and spent the better part of an afternoon composing a letter that she hoped might get a response from someone in his organization responsible for answering such benign requests.

To her surprise and delight, one week later she received a response from Bucky himself, stating, "I would like to take advantage of your offer to come work with us." Her letter had done a lot more than she had anticipated; she had expected to receive a mimeographed list of organizations to target for a job, but her letter put her in a position to work directly with one of the greatest twentieth-century thinkers.

Upon graduation, Amy Edmondson joined Bucky's staff and worked with him as a researcher and engineer for three years until he died suddenly a week before his eighty-eighth birthday. Her next career step was to author *A Fuller Explanation: The Synergetic Geometry of R. Buckminster Fuller* (Birkhauser, 1987) before being recruited to her current position as director of research and development, Pecos River Learning Centers, Inc., in Santa Fe, New Mexico. Here Amy is conducting research designed to understand the factors affecting adult learning in organizations, as well as curriculum research and development for this corporate learning center.

Amy's story is compelling, but what struck us particularly about the story was that Amy's dialogues with Bucky must have made her stand out in his mind—in spite of the thousands of people he spoke with each year. She heard him speak at MIT, Harvard, and on Nantucket—and was able to speak directly with him on the last two occasions. Through dialogue she established a connection, and that connection enriched her, expanded her horizons, and (although she wasn't job hunting at the time) even helped her land her first job out of college.

Dialogue is what this chapter is about: creating opportunities to interact with a wide range of people that you will get to know and who will get to know you, know how your mind works, experience your uniqueness, and develop a sense of how you might contribute to their company or organization. Through dialogue you are truly three-dimensional—and accomplish what no résumé, letter, proposal, or portfolio can accomplish on its own. Through dialogue you can engage a friend or former colleague or potential employer in an interaction that can help project you into their future.

Dialogue is the ultimate connecting link to your next job and career focus. Through your exploratory meetings, you will begin to hear about job possibilities or enter onto the scene at a point early enough so that you may not have to compete with others for a job. You will be able to respond to an unmet need within the organization.

That is why we believe that it is so essential in a job search to set up meetings with two people a day. That is, two dialogues with friends, former colleagues, industry leaders, referrals, or potential employers. Two people a day would mean 10 a week, 40 a month, and 120 in a three-month period of time. If you are setting up such exploratory meetings, plus engaging in all the rest of the mechanics of a good job search, you will become visible and your dialogues will start to pay off.

If you do your research prior to setting up exploratory interviews, you will have enough knowledge to have a dialogue on a number of subjects. Even in an actual job interview there should be give and take, dialogues which will give each of you a chance to evaluate the other regarding the appropriateness of the fit. Each meeting you have could be seen as a tennis game, with you taking your turn serving and receiving, and then relinquishing your serve to your opponent. This gives you both an opportunity at control—at deciding the focus of the conversation—as you uncover necessary data.

Planning—The Key to Successful Dialogues

The First Impression

As much as we don't want to admit it, first impressions in the job-search process can make or break your opportunities. As with the résumé or letter, a brilliant one will definitely not *get* you a job (though it could help you), but a terrible one—a sloppy one, one with even one typographical error, one with poor grammar or lacking clarity—can rule you out of the game in a split second.

The same is true with appearance. If you are dressed appropriately, in a suit and tie or dress and jacket that are up-to-date, in style, reflect the salary level you are targeting, the culture and dress of the company you are targeting, appearance will become a nonissue. But you may have difficulty impressing others if you:

- have clothes that are out of fashion or look worn or inexpensive—particularly if you are targeting a middle- or upper-level position.
- have clothes that are not impeccably groomed, or even one item of clothing that smells of smoke.
- have shoes or accessories that are unshined or worn.
- have gained or lost weight and have clothes that do not fit you well, and have neglected to purchase new clothing which does fit.
- have a hair style that hasn't been updated in several years or does not flatter you.
- have personal hygiene that is not impeccable—resulting in bad breath or body odor.
- have hands or fingernails that are not clean and well manicured.
- have glasses that are not currently in fashion or are very out-of-date.
- have ill-fitting contact lenses that cause you to squint.
- have a coat or raincoat that has become worn and doesn't reflect the level of the job you are targeting.
- have a briefcase or notebooks that are torn or worn and do not reflect the level of job you are targeting.

At first glance you may think dress concerns do not apply to you, believing that your appearance is beyond reproach. Look again and be brutally honest with yourself. A little investment in time and money now can make certain that you will not be eliminated from the running because you had clothes that smelled of smoke or body odor. It happens—and the true reason why you were eliminated will undoubtedly never be shared with you.

Planning for Self-Initiated (Exploratory) Meetings

After you've organized yourself to make an excellent first impression, you'll begin to spend a lot of time generating and then planning for self-initiated meetings, meetings you set up with a wide variety of people. You are about to become visible. You are clear about your options and directions and have generated a list of people who might be helpful to you in the coming weeks. You have even decided which former colleagues or friends you feel most comfortable calling first.

Now all you have to do is plan for the meeting you have set up for next Tuesday. How to plan is easy—just think about what results you want to achieve at the meeting, what you want to learn, what you want to leave the meeting having accomplished. You might be satisfied with the results of your meeting if:

- you brainstorm with a colleague about other possible jobs you could target—in addition to your own list.
- you come away with new companies or industries to target.
- you learn about what is going on in a company with which you were not well acquainted.
- you get help thinking about interim consulting you could do.
- you get other referrals within that company or within the community.
- your friend offers to call three people for you, to introduce you and to suggest they meet you for lunch.
- you have an opportunity to learn more about a new application for your talents in a different setting.
- you get new ideas on how to target the profit world if you are coming from not-for-profit, or vice versa.
- you learn about the process of establishing a consulting business and whether you should consider doing so.
- you find out about relevant books to read, journals to study, or association meetings to attend.
- you have opened the door to come back to this person for more leads, ideas, suggestions at a later date.

What you *do* want to do is show up at the meeting having carefully thought through how this person can help you, with appropriate marketing tools in your briefcase that are impeccable and well written, with clarity about the goals you want to accomplish, and having done adequate research about the company or industry you are exploring.

Being "In Process"

How can you be sure that your meetings have energy, have life? The best way is for you to go to the meeting with the goal of demonstrating yourself "in process." Look for ways to *show* how your mind works rather than just *telling* about your past or your future plans. Try to get the conversation focused on problems that need solving, unmet needs that must be addressed. Look for ways to establish a dialogue that really allows you to share how you think. And look for ways to actually "pay the person back" for his or her time. Is there something you can give back in exchange, so that the person can actually be grateful the meeting took place? You could think about what you have, in terms of information and ideas, that might be of benefit to them. You could listen carefully to problems that are brought up, and share what has worked for you in the past if you have dealt with similar problems. You could suggest a book or journal that might interest them, and mention it in your follow-up letter. Or you could include a photocopy of an article that relates to your conversation and which might be useful to the other person.

Charles had been director of community relations for a major university prior to finding himself in a job search. His previous positions had contributed to his tremendous skill in a variety of areas—running not-for-profit foundations, innovative programming and teaching at the college level, development of leadership training programs, and fund-raising and grantsmanship. During the first level of his job search he set up interviews with people who served on committees with him at various community agencies. One such person worked in a company Charles was attracted to, though he was not sure what the fit between his talents and their needs might be.

Charles came to the meeting with a functional résumé committed to memory, so that he could begin the meeting by reviewing his areas of expertise, and tentatively suggest ways his skills might fit the organization's needs. He came to the meeting with the idea that a high-level public relations job might be a possibility. By the time he had left the meeting, he had obtained information about a new division of the company that was just in the process of being created—one which would concentrate on expanding the concept of training and then look for markets for these new training products. This division was being headed up internally but would need new talent from outside the company as it expanded.

So what started from a basic exploratory meeting with a colleague from a volunteer advisory board was transformed into a discussion of an actual job possibility. What is particularly significant was that the job was in an area totally unrelated to what he *thought* might be the right fit. Though he had extensive background in new-program development and training, he had no idea this was a new thrust for the company—so he could never have suggested it. He trusted that if he demonstrated his areas of effectiveness, new ideas would emerge, as they did.

In most cases, you will want to conclude the meeting you have initiated with a request for other referral names. Asking for referrals is a necessary part of the job search, but one that is uncomfortable for most job searchers. After all, this person already gave you his or her time. Do you have a right to ask for referral names, or is that being too aggressive, expecting too much?

The problem is that you *need* the referral names. If the majority of the jobs out there are hidden, only to surface by your personally uncovering them, you have no choice but to ask for referral names. Now obviously, Charles would not ask for referral names, since he had actually uncovered a possibility. But when a meeting has not been that fruitful, you can conclude the meeting with the following request: "I would appreciate it if you would take a couple of minutes now and help me think of other people who might help direct me on my search or provide me with further information and ideas." And then wait, with the expectation that the names will be forthcoming. They usually are.

Often it helps if you ask specific questions to jog people's memories about who they know. You might say, "Is there anybody you see regularly at association meetings who might be helpful or particularly interesting to speak with?" Or you could stimulate recall simply by asking them to check an association membership list or their business card files. Or you might suggest ten companies that you would love to target, and ask whether they know anyone in those companies that you could call.

There seems to be a pattern to the success of job searchers in receiving referrals. It hinges on whether they feel justified in asking and actually *expect* the names to be forthcoming. If they ask in a confident manner, stating that they will not be calling these people for jobs but just for information, believing that it is not such a big deal to ask for a couple of names, they usually get the names. On the other hand, if they feel as if this is a major imposition and they have no right to ask for the names, they will often meet with resistance. What seems to determine success or failure is the degree to which the searcher actually feels justified in doing the asking. Attitude is all important.

Planning for Employer-Initiated Meetings—Job Interviews

The job interview. It has a formidable ring—so much is riding on the success or failure of your meeting with a potential employer. Many books have been written which claim they will prepare you for the interview. They tell you how to sit, what to wear, when to ask questions, and tell you what questions will most likely be asked. For some reason, though, these books often are not comforting, and the information does not assist you in becoming confident, in remembering how much you have to offer and how lucky the company would be if you chose to accept the position they offer.

In *The Inner Game of Tennis*, Timothy Gallwey introduces the concept of learning to play good tennis without trying to remember exactly how to hold the racquet or when to bend your knees or exactly how to pivot. As we mentioned earlier in the book, he pioneered a new method of teaching tennis, or more accurately, of assisting people in learning or improving their game without trying to remember all that cumbersome detail. The results have been astounding, and Gallwey has successfully translated his approach into learning other sports such as golf and skiing.

The book states that "neither mastery nor satisfaction can be found in the playing of any game without giving some attention to the relatively neglected skills of the inner game. This game takes place in the mind of the player and is played against such obstacles as lapses in concentration, nervousness, self-doubt, and self-condemnation. In short, it is played to overcome all habits of mind which inhibit excellence in performance."

Gallwey extols the value of relaxed concentration. He has demonstrated over and over again in his work with people that this is a true basis of self-confidence, that the secret in winning lies partly in not trying too hard. Gallwey talks about quieting the mind, allowing oneself to perform well rather than forcing it. The minute a tennis player begins to judge his playing—"That was a bad serve," or "That return was poorly done"—the player becomes preoccupied with the negatives, and the game starts to slip, along with his self-confidence.

If you would apply these concepts to the job interview and were able to enter a state of relaxed concentration, you would be able to allow all the preparation you had done for this meeting to surface in very natural ways. And you would not lose sight of what you want to communicate about yourself and what you need to learn about the position and the company. After you have prepared for this interview, you can sit back and *let* it happen. You can relax, because all your sensory-rich visualization exercises will have had their positive effect, and you will be able to confidently proceed.

You won't have to work at interviewing, occupying your mind with whether you are doing it properly. Your mind will be free to focus on the *content* of the conversation at hand, and so you will automatically be more effective.

The Nitty-Gritty—On
Connecting . . . Becoming Visible

Just like Casper the Ghost, you are invisible. But unlike Casper, you probably do not realize that the world cannot see you, so you are at a grave disadvantage. Oh you may think that you have "covered your bases," having listed your availability at your association, told your friends and neighbors about your company's downsizing and the dissolution of your department, and sent out a letter to a hundred friends and acquaintances.

Sure—that *is* a beginning. But think of all the people who could benefit from your special combination of talent and experience but would not know where or how to find you. In fact, it is extremely likely that they do not even believe you exist. Perhaps they have never come across anybody with your unique blend of background and experiences.

How do you become visible? We've spoken about it earlier in the book. Refer back to your list of people you know (see chapter 5) and begin to go systematically down that list, setting up meetings. Set up as many face-to-face connecting meetings as possible—as many as can be adequately prepared for and followed up on. Your goal for these meetings is not to be offered a position on the spot or even to hear about one that is open (although it will be wonderful when that happens). Your goals are to communicate your energy and enthusiasm about your area of interest, for you *both* to have gained from the experience, for new ideas to crop up in your mind, for you to take your thinking about possibilities for yourself one step further. When the other person has met you, talked with you, brainstormed with you—then you have become visible. Now he or she can think about whom you should meet or what other targets you might consider. You are adequately "known" and could be referred for potential jobs at this point.

An additional bonus of connecting is that through it you will have a better chance of hearing about job possibilities early enough on the time line so that you'll not always have to compete with others for jobs. For example, look at the following time line, which is designed to demonstrate the process of job development.

The Development of a Job

A	B	C	D	E	F	G

A. There is a problem or an unmet need in the company that no one is focusing on.
B. Someone recognizes a need in the company.
C. A discussion starts internally about this need.
D. A job description is developed.
E. A job is advertised.
F. Interviews are held.
G. A candidate is selected for the job.

Notice how a job developed many steps after someone within the company had recognized a need. If you had met in an exploratory meeting with the individual(s) in the company at point A or B, by the time the job description was written at point D, it might have been designed with you in mind. Entering early in this time line, you would have participated in the creation of your own job and saved the company the time and cost of advertising and interviewing candidates for the position. Additionally, you would not have had to compete with others for the job as you would have if you had entered the process at point E, when the job might have been advertised. The logic of this early entry into the process is especially helpful to see for job searchers who may tend to think of networking or exploratory meetings as having less value or importance than job interviews.

Multiple Contacts—The
Name of the Game

If you have ever been in a position to hire people yourself, take a moment to recall the process you went through. Do you remember the job searcher who took initiative and sent not only a follow-up letter but an article that related to your conversation? And then do you remember his calling and requesting a lunch meeting to further explore some of the ideas that came up? Do you remember feeling as if you trusted him more as you got to know him better?

It stands to reason that one variable that plays a significant role in being hired is that of being known—being familiar. If you have recommendations that opened doors, if you have multiple contacts during the search, if you have been active in the community or visible in other ways, it feels safer to hire you. So as the job searcher, you'll want to look for ways to become more familiar to those doing the hiring, so that they can get comfortable with the idea of hiring you. By the time they offer you the job, you will want them to feel as if they really know you.

Is the Phone Ringing?

Picture this "would be" scene from a Hollywood film classic. Oscar has just been informed that his job is being discontinued, that his division is being dissolved, and that he is out of a job. He is informed about his severance package, and told to clean out his desk immediately, return home, and discuss the entire situation with his family.

That same evening, while the family is preparing to eat dinner, the telephone starts ringing; many of his cohorts are calling to see how he is doing, to see if there is any way they can help him. Some offer names of company presidents who are good friends. Others have recent excellent résumés that they offer to share with him for format ideas. Still others have good contacts with executive recruiters in New York, Chicago, and San Francisco, his favorite cities.

Oscar's job transition begins with the telephone ringing, and it literally rings off the hook throughout his entire job search. His family rallies around him, reassuring him at crucial moments of his worth, of his excellent experience, of his outstanding credentials. These messages are echoed throughout by his peers, business associates, and former employers.

People he meets with call every once in a while to see how his search is proceeding. Recruiters call with possibilities for him and reassure him that options are opening up. Company presidents, friends of friends, continue checking back with him to let him know when something looks as if it is becoming a possibility. All this occurs without his ever having to initiate any phone calls or contacts himself.

The scene fades.

Enough. It is not that this picture is absurd or impossible. It is just that from what we have seen with our clients, the scenario is quite unrealistic to say the least. Many people will be willing and eager to help you during your search, but the initiative will most likely be yours, the telephone calls will be those that you initiate, the follow-up calls your idea. Others will need help knowing how they can assist you. You'll need to guide them.

Is the Phone Covered?

If you are not going to be sitting home waiting for the phone to ring, who is? As we mentioned in our discussion of the phone number to put on your résumé, you may want to use an answering service to forward your calls to when no one is home.

But what if you share your phone with the rest of your family, including some teenagers, or children under age five? You wouldn't want your teenage son switching the call-waiting device on the phone (if you have it) and answering a call to you from a potential employer as if he were speaking to one of his buddies, or to ignore the call-waiting beep altogether. Recruiters and employers have a habit of calling anytime, day or night.

You'll probably want to set up a family meeting and discuss the importance of members answering the phone more formally during the duration of your job search. If they understand their livelihood also depends on your success, your children may be more than willing to cooperate with you. It may be a good idea to role-play with the family members who have access to the phone about just what they will say *every time* they answer the phone.

Other options include having a special phone line installed during your job search, forwarding your calls when you are out to a friend, neighbor, or relative's home, or using a good-quality answering machine programmed with your own voice. Whoever takes your messages, make sure that they take careful, complete notes so that you will have the correct spelling of the person's name and an accurate phone number including area code. Attention to these details will save you grief and aggravation and will mean that you will not lose an opportunity unnecessarily.

Cold Calls/Warm Calls

Let us say that there is this one person that you would like to meet. You have exhausted all of your personal network, and nobody knows this person. But you have read about him in the local business news and have a hunch that meeting him would be good for your job-search campaign. How do you get to him, and how can you convert this cold call to a warm call?

For those of you who have not been in sales, thinking about making a "cold call" might send shivers up your spine. Why else would it be called a cold call? How do you get beyond the uncomfortable feelings that you have when making cold calls? One way is to think about them as "warm calls." You can start by changing your expectation of response from one of probable rejection to one of probable acceptance. Visualize the person on the other end of the line smiling, listening, nodding at what you say, and agreeing to meet. Consider others lucky that you have identified them as the ones you want to meet. And expand your concept of warm calls to include the secretaries, whom until now you have perceived as "foe" rather than "friend."

Making telephone calls to set up appointments might not be so bad if you didn't have to "get through the secretary." You know what we mean, because perhaps you have taken great care to train your own secretary to "screen out" unwanted callers. She may have become quite proficient at meeting your needs, interrupting you only when you would want an interruption, and for those calls that she felt confident you would like to accept. As a matter of fact, you did your job of training her so well that she learned to take a good number of calls for you, refer them to other departments, or state that you did not have time for such calls.

Did you ever stop to think, to wonder about those calls that *did* penetrate her competent blockade? Sometimes they were not ones you cared to accept, but they made it through, and you found yourself talking to a potential vendor, a college administrator seeking new markets, or a job seeker.

We've worked with secretaries who are involved with upgrading their skills, expanding their job definitions, returning to college for degrees, or planning for job and career changes. An exceedingly large proportion of these secretaries are talented, smart, dedicated, introspective, and striving to achieve something within their too often repetitive, and unappreciated jobs. They will respond under the right conditions.

If you are curt or distant or communicate by your words or tone of voice that you believe her to be unimportant or beneath you, chances are she will screen you right out. But if you perceive her as a potential ally, as an important part of the connecting process, as someone who can just as easily choose to help you as to hinder you, you will begin to see your successes skyrocket. After all, she may be just the individual who can help you strategize about when would be best to connect with him. She may be searching for ways to expand her job, to stretch her brain, to prove herself.

To speak to her in a manner that says, "I am certain that you are extremely intelligent, and you deserve a concise description of why I want to connect with your boss, and I respect you enough to speak to you in the same way I would like to be spoken to," will gain you significant mileage in your job-search process. We've had clients tell us that on their third or fourth call, by which time they were on a friendly first-name basis with the secretary, she would go out of her way to be helpful—and to pin down a time when the boss could be reached.

If the person you are trying to reach is not able to take your call, it is best to tell the secretary that you'd rather not play telephone tag and that you will call him back since you are hard to reach (which is true if you are having your daily exploratory meetings). In this way, especially if the person you are calling doesn't know you, you will be saving the secretary the aggravation of trying to explain to her boss why he should return your call. You also retain the control and the opportunity of calling again, whenever the secretary suggests would be a good time.

Who Are You Afraid to Call?

Who is on your list that you are reluctant or anxious about calling? You can think of many good reasons why he or she wouldn't want to be bothered or why it is inappropriate for you to place that call.

Paul was a vice president of a corporation when he found himself downsized right out of a job. His career had been on the fast track up to that point, and along the way he had accumulated several advanced degrees including a law degree and an M.B.A. He had few contacts in his geographical area, having relocated back to his hometown after being away a number of years.

One resource he had, if he could become comfortable accessing it, was his high school graduating class. But it was twenty-five years since he had seen or spoken to most of these folks, and he felt uncomfortable and embarrassed to be contacting members of the class when he was in need, when he hadn't chosen to connect with them otherwise. But he swallowed his pride and made the calls. His former classmates were extremely supportive—and impressed with his educational background and experience. They helped him brainstorm various possibilities—familiarizing him with companies and opportunities that were unknown to him. His next job came through one of these contacts, who actually hired him to work in his company.

What do you imagine is the *very* worst thing that could happen if you called up someone you think is too busy to speak with you or who you believe would be uninterested in helping you out? Do you think they would say, "You dumb [expletive]! What gives you the right to call me up and ask me for help? You are merely a lowly controller, and I am a high-class company president—and I definitely have no time for the likes of you! So scram!"? Or do you imagine the following response: "You must really be a loser to be out of a job! I can definitely understand why you would want my help, but unfortunately my life is too filled with important and meaningful things and I have no time for you!"?

You get the drift. It isn't even a bad idea to let your imagination run wild. Actually say out loud and write down *exactly* what you fear the person on the other end of the telephone would say to you. In our experience the following is the worst that job searchers have experienced: "I'm sorry that I am so busy for the next couple of months. I wish I had the time to help you, but I have a project that prevents me from taking any time away from the job just now."

So the very worst thing that will happen is for you to get a polite refusal. Maybe you won't like the tone of voice the other person uses. But that is a small price to pay for the *possibility* that you might actually generate a meeting. And of course the chances of generating a meeting are quite high if you get in the name of the person who referred you—probably about 90 percent in your favor.

What to Say on the Telephone

What you say on the telephone will vary depending on who you are calling and the specific purpose of the call. You'll need to vary your strategy depending on the category of person with whom you are speaking.

Calls to Friends
and Relatives and Colleagues

To these folks you can state that you are in the process of a job search and would like to meet with them to brainstorm about possibilities with which they might be familiar, and about which you would like to learn. You can say that you'd like to show them your résumé, talk to them about your areas of interest, and just put your heads together to see what you can come up with. If any of them work at corporations that interest you at all, you can brainstorm with them about where you might fit in the organizations if there were a need—and perhaps get some referral names to follow up on those ideas. You'll be certain to assure these folks that you don't expect them to know of a job opening, but that through talking with them, you hope to get some new ideas.

Calls to Referrals from Friends, Relatives, and Colleagues

When you get a referral name, it is absolutely crucial to get more information about that person than just his or her name. Ask about the person's title and function within the organization, about anything that makes the person stand out; ask for more specifics about why they might be helpful to you. Take notes when you are given the referral and have the notes in front of you when you are making the call.

Then when you call, you can say, "Jerry Jackson suggested that I call you. I know Jerry from the days when we were both design engineers together, but I have moved on to management, as I know you have, too. I am currently in a job transition and looking to identify a place where I can make a contribution. Jerry felt that you and I had a lot in common and that you could be particularly helpful to me in evaluating opportunities in the local market. He mentioned to me that he thought you had initiated several job changes in the last few years yourself, and felt that I could learn a thing or two from speaking with you. Could I meet you for breakfast next Tuesday or Wednesday?"

The conversation is personalized—it doesn't seem like you pulled his name out of a hat or found it in a telephone book, but it is clear that you are intentional about who you are calling and why you are placing the call.

When you call the referral names, you are not ever expecting that they will have or even know of a job opening. You are not looking for a "slot" but want to find out where there might be a need for someone with your skills and expertise. If there were an opening, someone who did not know you wouldn't tell you about it anyway. After all, at that point you are a total unknown, and you wouldn't find out unless you seemed to be an outstanding candidate. Then they might tell you, at the end of the exploratory meeting. If there were about to be a restructuring, they wouldn't tell you. If someone were about to be promoted out of the department, leaving a position in the department, they wouldn't tell you unless they knew you. So your best bet is to assume that there might be a need—but know that they will never tell you unless they have met you and are impressed.

When you go to your exploratory meetings, you are looking for information, feedback, ideas, brainstorming opportunities, and of course, unmet needs and problems to solve. If you uncover actual opportunities right there in the company—terrific. If not, you have a new contact, and if the meeting is particularly good, you might have an actual supporter who will demonstrate interest in your progress throughout your search.

Frank had been a laborer in a warehouse, a key spokesman in the union, a warehouse assistant manager, and then an assistant plant manager. While he was working he went to college at the company's expense and completed a degree in industrial relations. His years of experience in representing labor to management were invaluable in his understanding of labor-management problems. He had a wonderful reputation for fair negotiation and was an outstanding communicator.

Then Frank was fired, and he found himself in a job search. He found it difficult to explore positions in labor relations since he had never before held an actual management job in that area. So he geared his search toward plant management instead. He could never quite get comfortable with doing exploratory interviewing for information. He deeply believed that he would never get a job offer in labor relations because he had never held the job before.

Well, he had to start somewhere. If he had been a young college graduate in labor relations, he would have had to start from the beginning. He had credentials that far surpassed what a college grad would have, but his belief system prevented him from setting up those meetings. His personal contacts were limited, and his referral source seemed to dry up. So he would have had to do some direct targeting and "warm calling" to directors of human resources and directors of labor relations in order to generate activity. If he identified ten people to call and only one or two agreed to see him, he would have steered the search in a new direction. If he had made those calls, he could have said something such as the following:

My name is Frank Simpson, and I read about you in the *Labor Relations Journal*. My background is in warehouse and plant management, as well as union negotiations from the labor end. I am in the process of conducting a job search in the labor relations area and would love the opportunity to come by and meet with you for twenty or twenty-five minutes, to find out about how labor relations works in your company and how it might have compared to labor relations at my previous place of employment. Could we meet sometime next week?

Now, is that dishonest? Not at all. He *did* want to learn more about how labor relations works in this company. He *was* interested in comparing it to where he had been. He really did not know enough about similar departments in different companies and needed to learn more in order to begin to get a clear picture about where he could fit.

Likewise, having several such meetings like this would help you clarify your thinking and let you dispel your beliefs that you would never get a job in an area without having had direct experience.

If a referral says to you, "We don't have any openings," you simply have to assume that he needs more clarification regarding the purpose of your call. You could reply with, "Well, it would have been too coincidental that just when I call you, there is an opportunity. I did not expect that you would have an opening. I am looking for information, perspective, and ideas. Would you help me so that I can develop an outstanding job search?"

At the Exploratory
Meetings—What to Do

Remember to use your functional résumé when meeting people you don't know. Walking someone through your résumé is a marvelous way to begin and sets you up as a well-prepared, organized person who has carefully thought through your specific strengths and areas of expertise. Many meetings will begin with the person you are meeting with asking you, "So what can I do for you?"

Now the ball is in your court. One effective way to begin a meeting is for you to summarize your areas of effectiveness that are listed on your functional résumé. You can do it from memory—or you can pull out your résumé and say something like, "It might save us time if you glance at my functional résumé to get a quick picture of my areas of effectiveness. *I want to reiterate that I certainly don't expect that you have a job.* I'm using this résumé as a quick way to convey my talents to you."

The director of community relations that we mentioned earlier in the chapter took his functional résumé on an exploratory meeting and said, "I'm so pleased to be here because I have such high regard for this company. If you look at my areas of effectiveness, you'll see that my expertise lies in program design and training, development and fund-raising, and public relations and community affairs. One possible fit for my skills in a company like this would be in the public relations area. But I am really open to new ideas. Based on these areas of expertise, what comes to mind that might also be a good fit?"

And that is how this client opened the door in his exploratory meeting to his eventually being hired in a position that hadn't yet even been created, as manager of a new external training function—by being open and honest about his expertise and not feeling as if he had to know all the possibilities prior to going to the meeting. He *did* need to know about his own strengths and skills, but he did not need to know every possible job title out there. That would be an impossible task, and since every company operates differently, it is literally impossible to know.

After each meeting you have, you'll want to do careful follow-up. Each person you meet with should receive a letter that is more than just a perfunctory thank-you (see chapter 4). And you'll want to establish some careful controls so that you can begin to track your activities. Some job searchers like to fill out call sheets, as salespersons do, stating the results of the meeting and the names of referrals from each person at that meeting. You also might like to consider creating a mind map of all the referrals you receive. You can create a system to keep track of what referrals you have followed up on by using a certain color marker to outline the ones you have already seen.

One of your great frustrations in your job search may be that there is no proof that you are accomplishing anything unless you are getting offers. You may feel as if "nothing is happening." And by that you mean that you haven't gotten offers yet. Well, all you need is one good offer, and you know job searches take anywhere from six weeks to six or seven months. So if you develop some methods to see at a glance what you have accomplished, whom you have seen, what resulted from each of those meetings, at least you'll have visual proof that you have been working hard.

If you have ever sold large computer systems or heavy equipment or investment properties or put together a merger or an acquisition, you know that a deal can often take from six months to a year to consummate. You are now selling a major "item"—*you*—and it may take a few months to finalize what will ultimately be a wonderful opportunity. Your job throughout that process is to find ways to feel as if you are building toward that goal—and to reassure yourself that you are not wasting time.

Connecting with Headhunters

In a self-initiated job search, the headhunters are still very much out there. They are still searching to fill positions assigned exclusively to them from their client companies (if they are retainer

recruiters) or wanting to participate in placement but competing with other agencies (if they are contingency recruiters).

So now's the time to pick up the telephone and call every recruiter who ever called you or whom you used to hire people yourself or is suggested by colleagues or is advertising positions in professional or trade journals in your field. Naturally, you are aware that the chance that a recruiter may be working on a search that exactly matches your qualifications is slim. But (re)establishing contact can't hurt—and might open up a door otherwise closed to you. An updated résumé in his files will be important, in case anyone in the agency is working on a search for someone with your background and skills.

It is important to remember that recruiters will be looking for a perfect fit between your talents and the job they have to fill. They will hardly ever be open to making a recommendation that does not look like a perfect fit. So save your creative job-search scenarios for everyone else and use the recruiter only for uncovering possibilities that you are, beyond a shadow of a doubt, qualified to target.

Many recruiters do specialize in certain industries. So if you are in health care, first you'll want to contact all the recruiters specializing in health care. (You will find them listed by industry and geographically in the several available directories of recruiters, some of which advertise in journals in your field.) Send each a letter and a résumé, carefully targeted to one or more individuals at the firm, including the senior partner and the director of research. Then follow up each mailing with a telephone call and an attempt to speak directly with someone who handles searches similar to yours. Sometimes you'll be referred to the director of research, who should be handled with as much finesse and respect as you would demonstrate if talking with the senior partner. Hopefully, some of these calls and mailings will uncover either a contingency recruiter who believes in you, or a retainer recruiter who is handling a search for which you are qualified.

The Job Interview—What Are They Really Asking?

Each person with whom you interview will have his or her own style. If you are meeting with human resources or personnel professionals, you may experience some similarity in their approaches. But if you are interviewing with the person to whom you will report—who has no "formal" training in interviewing—you will experience a radically different approach to the process.

If asked, company presidents or senior-level people who are often charged with interviewing would tell you that they'd rather be doing *anything* else. They know they have a need, but it seems so tedious sometimes to have to talk to a number of people, sift through their backgrounds and experience, and identify whether or not there is a fit. They often get nervous about the need to make a choice, never knowing for sure whether you are *really* the one to help them solve their problems or remedy their unmet needs. Many admit that they do not really trust themselves to uncover adequate information or to evaluate what they have uncovered. There is often difficulty getting adequate references due to the fear that companies now have about potential litigation against them. So more and more of the responsibility falls on the shoulders of the interviewer, who must be in a position to make a decision that will benefit the company long-term.

Now, granted, in many cases a number of people will interview you so that a number of points of view about your background and experience can be shared. Even when you are being interviewed by a series of individuals, however, you'll often be speaking with interviewers who have no special training in the process, and who may well wish they were elsewhere at that moment.

The questions in the back of the minds of interviewers are always going to be: "What can this person do for us? Can he or she help us solve our problems? Is he or she the one who can get us back on track or up to speed? Is he or she a good problem solver, the right one to help us put these new programs together or create these new systems?"

In other words, *What can you do for them? Why have you been successful and how did you do it? What makes you tick? How can you make a difference in the bottom line, on the balance sheet?* By the end of the interview they should be able to answer these questions easily. You'll want to be looking for ways to help them get those answers, *even if they don't ask the right questions.* Naturally each person you speak with will have his or her own style. Some will begin by telling you all about the company and letting you get comfortable. Others will begin with the question, "Why would you like to work for this company?" and will be looking for any initiative you took in your research that allows you to answer this question well. Some interviewers will be more swayed by style than substance—if they feel comfortable with you and like you, you'll have a good shot at the position. Others will be much more rational and objective, sticking to the facts about what is needed and carefully scrutinizing your background to see if there is a match.

So what are your goals at a job interview? You want to demonstrate a positive attitude, high energy and spirit, enthusiasm and excitement about the opportunity. Richard Bolles, author of *What Color Is Your Parachute?* (Ten Speed Press, 1989), believes that energy and enthusiasm about future opportunities is of immeasurable importance. You will be attractive if you are excited. Now is not the time to play it cool, but rather to clearly show it if you are nearly jumping out of your skin at an opportunity. Now we're not talking about being "needy" or "hungry," which does tend to turn others off. We're not talking about what you need but what you want and are drawn toward.

It's funny, but much of the time we spend with clients is spent curing their amnesia. It's not uncommon for us to work with someone skilled in mergers and acquisitions who neglects to negotiate a good contract for himself. Likewise it is not uncommon for someone comfortable in dialogues with CEOs and company presidents to regress into an "obedient" manner of responding when in job interviews, even if this person previously had been responsible for significant high-level recruiting himself. So it becomes our job to remind you about what you already know, to remind you how smart you are, to help you remember high-level interactions you've had and the number of interviews you yourself have conducted in the past ten years. It becomes a priority for you to get back in touch with what you already know—and resist falling into the trap of behaving like a "job searcher" looking for *Robert's Rules of Order* as they relate to the job interview. We'd like to encourage you to be authentic—the very antithesis of what many

job-search books will recommend. All the research you have done about yourself and about the potential job will pay off at this point, while you are searching for a mutual fit.

Now is the time for you to realize that if you do get hired, nobody is doing you a favor. You will be hired because they *need* you. This business of job interviewing should not be one way, with them doing the evaluating and you being evaluated. Rather it must be a two-way interchange, an exchange of ideas and information. It should be an exploration of a possible fit between your talents and their needs. Throughout the interviews, remind yourself of how lucky *they* would be to hire you to help them. Picture yourself interviewing them—asking good questions, scrutinizing the responses, proposing new ideas, looking for a mutual fit. If you come from this position of strength in your thinking, you will counteract appearing "needy." The truth is you both have needs—and that is what you are there to explore.

Now, it might make sense for you to have a couple of conversations with a friend and even to audiotape or, if possible, videotape the process. When you listen to or observe yourself, you may find an obvious problem that up until now you haven't been particularly aware of. One client, for example, heard himself say the word "like" thirty-eight times in one thirty-minute taped conversation. Another client discovered that he spoke too fast, and made a conscious effort to slow down his speech during the interview process. If you listen to yourself on tape, you can work to eliminate annoying speech habits that might prevent others from seeing your talents at a first or second meeting.

What You Are Moving Toward?

A key point to remember is that you will want to present yourself in terms of what you are moving toward, not what you are moving away from. The answer to any question that asks you why you left, what you didn't like about your previous position, why you were fired should incorporate the truth (as you see it) about what you are moving toward. If you remember to focus on that, you'll never accidentally get caught in bad-mouthing a previous employer or company. You'll be proactive and purposeful, reflecting your future goals rather than your past.

The Question Behind
the Question

Let's assume that you have prepared well, thoroughly researched a company, familiarized yourself with similarities between this industry and the industry with which you are most familiar, visualized the experience as being positive, brought your portfolio, reviewed your résumé, and now you feel really excited about the meeting. You are aware that the first contact is probably not sufficient for an offer, but this will lead to the next step. You are prepared to learn something from the experience—not just focus on whether you are "winning" or not.

And then come the unexpected questions. Ones you forgot you

would be asked: "Why did you get fired?" "You seem to have changed jobs a lot. To what do you attribute this?" "What types of people do you have difficulty getting along with?" "You have no familiarity with this industry except for your exposure during your job search. Don't you believe this would be a liability in the position for which you are interviewing?" "You worked for a very large corporation with lots of perks and a lucrative stock option plan. Do you believe you would be satisfied with our plan, which is meager in comparison?" "How do you feel about reporting to someone younger than you?"

Some questions could be initially perceived as trick questions, calculated to make you squirm, or they could simply be questions that, although asked inexpertly, indicate a valid concern held by the questioner. With a perspective that the interviewer is a potential ally rather than an adversary, it is easier to react positively to seemingly difficult or tricky questions. And the best strategy is to answer the question *behind* the question, rather than merely answering the question itself.

For example, the question "Why have you changed industries three times?" could be really asking the question "I wonder if he could be effective coming into our industry without the background that someone else might have in it?" Your goal is to respond to the questions behind the surface question, and you might say, "I have always been attracted to new bodies of knowledge and new areas, wanting to grow and develop my mind while still doing my job well. I find that I am a quick learner and am attracted to this high-tech field partly because it will allow me to expand my knowledge base in this area." In this case the move to a new industry reflects an innate curiosity and attraction to new areas, rather than a failure in previous ones.

What's important is for you to carefully think through why you made each of the changes you made and be able to present positive, honest reasons why the moves were advantageous for you over the long term. If you've successfully answered the questions that lurk behind the questions, you'll be on track.

Behind the question "What types of people do you have difficulty getting along with?" might be the question "Can you work with blue-collar and noncollege-educated workers as effectively as you can work with CEOs and sales managers?" or "Would you fit into our company culture—where everyone is expected to answer the telephone if customer service is busy, so that it never rings more than three times?" Obviously you've given some thought to what kinds of people you work best with, and whom you don't effectively work with. If you've done your homework on the company and on the job, you'll be able to gear your answer to what you think might be on the interviewer's mind.

The question "Don't you think a director of marketing should have direct industry experience?" might be asking, "Would you be at a disadvantage because you're coming into a high-tech industry with no background in the area." You can respond to this concern by talking about the transferability of your skills, about the outstanding successes in marketing where newcomers were not experienced in the industry.

John Sculley, who was recruited by Apple Computer from Pepsi and who had no background in computers, is a perfect example. Sculley had a very technical mind, an interest in learning the industry, and a brilliant marketing mind. Although he had not sought this job, obviously Steve Jobs was not concerned that he was coming from outside the industry. He was looking for a brilliant mind and an outstanding marketer to help put Apple on the map in the minds of American consumers.

"You've worked for a large conglomerate for the last twenty years. Why do you think you could be happy at a small entrepreneurial organization like ours?" is a question looming more and more on the minds of potential employers. What they are really asking are questions like "Do you really know how to work hard?" "Are you used to having layers of people do the work for you?" "Is your knowledge obsolete, or are you current?" "Can you make decisions quickly, or have you succumbed to the slow pace of a large bureaucracy?" "Do you know what it is like to roll up your sleeves and dig in to get the job done?" So when you hear the first question, you immediately think about what he really wants to know, and go about the business of answering the underlying questions.

"How do you feel about working for a younger person . . . a woman . . . a young company president . . . a black or a Hispanic?" The questions behind these questions include: "Will your prejudice prevent you from getting the job done?" "Will you fit into our company culture?" "Will you be effective in our industry, which markets primarily to minority markets?" So think through what you really feel about the responses to these questions. Look for specific examples from throughout your work history with which to punctuate your story, and assure your interviewer that these would not be problems for you. If you can build a case that you see any potential problem as a challenge, an opportunity for growth, so much the better.

What about the questions "What is your worst fault?" or "What is your biggest mistake?" or "What is your Achilles heel?" or "What is your major liability?" In each of these instances, the interviewer is trying to get a handle on you—to see through any veneer, to learn what makes you tick. He's looking for information which will either screen you in or screen you out. If you are impatient with people who are not committed to getting the job done, you can tell the truth about your imperfections while still reflecting strength of conviction.

If you are approaching each interviewer as a potential ally, you will not be judging each question as to its merit. If you do that, you might regress into negative and defensive responses, which will work against you. But if you approach each question as an opportunity to tell the truth and be authentic, as a chance to give specific examples and let the interviewer in on your uniqueness, you'll be creating a positive experience. You'll want to remind yourself that even when a question seems argumentative or irrelevant, or even possibly illegal, the interviewer usually believes that he has a right and valid reason to ask it. And you'll try to imagine what the interviewer really wants to know—and then answer those underlying concerns.

Questions You May Be Asked

Following is a list of questions to help you begin to prepare for job interviews. Since they are of a very general nature, we urge you to individualize them for your particular situation, and to give some thought to how you might answer each of them. An advantage of thinking through your responses is that you will then be protected from being caught off guard. You'll have thought through responses to sensitive questions and can then help propel the dialogue into one of mutual exchange, where you each learn enough about the other to make an informed decision about any potential fit. The list is not meant to be all-inclusive, merely to get you started on thinking through possible questions you may be asked.

One hint to remember is not to drone on and on in response to a particular question. Answer with a carefully conceived, brief response, and check to see if the interviewer wants more, wants you to go into greater depth, and if you are responding with the information he or she wants.

1. Can you tell me about your educational background, from your decision to go to college, through graduate school or specialized training? (If you did not attend college, think through why not, where your "formal education" came from, and even prepare some examples of people in your field who are highly visible and successful—and did it without a college degree.)

2. Would you discuss your work history, beginning with your earliest job and working forward to the present? (Be prepared to explain gaps in your work history, since high on the employer's mind at this time are negligent hiring laws making them liable for the actions of all of their employees.)

3. Why did you leave your last job? Why were you fired? Why have you changed jobs so often? Why did you sell your company? Why were you not retained in some other capacity after the merger? Was the other MIS manager

more competent than you? Did it come as a surprise when you were fired, or did you anticipate it? How are your relations with your former employer? Explain.

4. What kinds of problems are you most attracted to solving? Give some examples of problems you solved successfully and ones you did not successfully resolve. Explain why not.

5. Is there anything on your résumé that you did not personally accomplish, but that you actually accomplished rather as a part of a team effort?

6. Have you done any hiring or firing? How do you approach the task? Are you good at choosing new hires? Support what you have to say.

7. What are the most difficult problems your last company had to face? How has the changing economy affected that industry or company? How do you project that the global economy will affect it in the next 5 to 10 years?

8. All companies have people problems. Which ones did you have in your previous job? Which ones caused serious repercussions? What did you try to do about them? In what instances were you successful? In what instances unsuccessful? Why?

9. What do you think of Tom Peters's *In Search of Excellence* (Warner, 1984) and Ken Blanchard's *One-Minute Manager* (Morrow, 1982) and John Naisbitt and Patricia Aburdene's *Re-inventing the Corporation* (Warner, 1985)? Did you adapt any of their principles on the job? Why or why not? Did they work?

10. What is your view on the development of the human resources in a company? Explain?

11. What are companies going to have to do to get a competitive edge in this industry? Substantiate your reply.

12. What is your view on customer service? How has the computer revolution affected it? Does customer service apply to your industry or organization? Explain.

13. What are your personal goals? Where do you want to be in 3 to 5 years? Why?

14. What steps are you taking for lifelong learning? Are you studying or learning any new area at the moment? What books have you read or what classes have you taken that you believe will enhance your marketability? Explain.

15. What is your view on community service? To what extent have you been involved in community service? How do you feel you'd fit with our corporate focus in this area? Do you think the corporation has a right to expect community service from its employees?

16. Why do you want to work here? What could you help us with? What is unique about you that would make a significant contribution to our bottom line?

17. What are we *not* doing here that you think we should be doing, based on your research into our organization? How should we go about changing our direction and improving our corporate goals?

18. Would you be willing to develop a proposal for the new job we've been discussing and back it up with specific recommendations as well as a budget? How long would it take you to put together such a proposal?

19. How do you feel about working in a culture like ours? How does it compare to the previous cultures you've worked in? What is your work ethic? How does that fit in with your commitment to your family and yourself?

20. How do you feel about travel? About relocating? About taking a job at less money than you were making previously? About working nights and weekends during certain projects? About company celebrations and employee exchanges? About working for a woman? About working for someone younger than you and without as much education as you have?

21. For every item on your résumé, be prepared to answer the questions "How did you do it?" and "Who did it benefit?" Be prepared to be specific, give examples. Be prepared with exact numbers, figures, percentages that you have memorized, if possible.

22. What is your management style? (Be prepared to support your answer with examples. Be prepared to show off the knowledge of the company that you have acquired through your research.)

23. Be prepared to respond to the request, "Tell me about your professional experience" or "Tell me about yourself" as it applies to the company or job you are targeting. (Be careful not to be long-winded. Keep your answers focused and brief; if the interviewer wants more, he or she will ask for more.)

24. If asked the question "What are you looking for?" don't get too specific. Talk about areas of expertise and general skills and how they will benefit the company. Don't lock yourself out of opportunities.

25. Think about how you plan to answer questions that are illegal—questions about your religion, national origin, spouse or children, or age.

How to Respond to Illegal Questions

You may want to be aware that questions that are not related to job requirements—regarding your national origin, political beliefs, religion, status of your spouse or children—are all illegal. Also illegal are questions relating to your age: when you were born, how old your children are, whether you are married or divorced, what your maiden name was, whether your spouse works, what kind of work your spouse does, whether you have arranged for child care, whether you plan to become pregnant. If you are asked an illegal question, you have three options: 1) answer the question; 2) state that you're wondering how the question relates to your ability to do the job for which you are interviewing; or 3) file a formal complaint with the EEOC.

But we do advise you to honestly assess your liabilities in the interview process. Let's face it—ageism and sexism do still exist. So does prejudice against handicapped individuals and the foreign born. In preparation for your interviews you might want to give some serious thought about how to translate into a real advantage something that someone else, due to hidden prejudices, might perceive as a liability.

Of course a key to making this kind of approach work in your favor is *your* believing that this so-called liability (your sex, your lack of degrees, your age) is really not a liability at all, but rather a real indication of your personal strength. If you believe that you have more to sell—many more years of experience and wisdom—as a result of being fifty-seven, if you are not feeling apologetic about being "too old" but instead are proud of who you are as a result of your age, you'll find it easier to transmit those feelings either directly or indirectly.

But They Have a Hiring Freeze

What exactly does that mean? Does it mean that the personnel department has been told that until future notification, they will not be advertising any jobs or doing any formal hiring? But even so, what about those who are planning next week to accept a job elsewhere, thereby leaving an opening? Or what about those who may be promoted next week, creating an opportunity for someone else? Or what about the spouse of an employee who decides to accept a promotion in another state, thus creating a vacancy? Or what about the restructuring that will take place in a month, producing a new division and needing new talent?

It is not all that uncommon for job searchers to get jobs where there is, in fact, a hiring freeze. One company did a major downsizing, had a hiring freeze besides, and still hired a full-time organizational development manager to help rebuild morale in two of the subsidiary divisions. Another company with a hiring freeze responded to a client's proposal to bring the recruiting function in-house and save them up to $150,000 a year merely by reducing dependence on external recruiters. A university with a freeze on hiring brought in a full-time, one-year external consultant to help reevaluate the admissions policies and create new systems to recruit students. So don't reduce your efforts to connect within companies that have hiring freezes. You never know where it might lead you.

Wally Armbruster, author of *Where Have All the Salesmen Gone?* (Wally Armbruster, Inc., 1982), a wonderfully irreverent book ("mainly for people in marketing and advertising, but helpful to everyone who has something to sell—a product, a dream, or a point of view"), tells a true story that demonstrates this business of the hiring freeze.

When Wally was the creative director of a very large and successful advertising agency in St. Louis, Missouri, a young copywriter named Steve had secured an interview with Wally through the business manager. Now, Wally had no interest in meeting with Steve but felt obligated because the appointment had already been arranged.

When Steve introduced himself, he stated unequivocally that he was not just in search of a job—he had a good one—he was in search of a job working for Wally, ever since he had heard him lecture at his university journalism class.

He flat-out said, up front, "Now, I don't expect you to hire me after one interview—one advertisement—but I've learned that campaigns are the secret to good selling. So I just want you to know that I'm going to keep coming back, with more and more evidence that you should hire me, until I get the job." (Note: That's what we are suggesting you do—go back with more and more evidence that whoever you are targeting needs you and should offer you a job. Only, we're not suggesting that you actually say out loud what Steve said.)

Next Steve handed Wally a list of Wally's clients (he had done his research) and proceeded to pull items from a bag—products for which Wally's agency had developed advertising campaigns—and related his life experience with each of them. He followed this "show and tell" with a portfolio of his own created ads, explaining his participation in each and even some of the ideas he'd had which weren't accepted. (Wally liked Steve's ideas best, even those that had been rejected.)

Now, what was going on as Wally was listening? He was impressed, but he still wanted Steve to leave, because the company was in a firing, not a hiring, mode.

Now, Steve's response—without a moment of hesitation—was to say that he was certain that since the agency was so outstanding, it would turn around in no time and would need more people than ever. In the meantime he planned to work on his next advertisement to demonstrate his talent, and he wanted to know at that point just exactly what doubts Wally had about his ability.

Wally told him that a sense of humor was missing from the ads, and Steve practically jumped for joy at that feedback. A couple of days later Wally opened his mail to find a Polaroid picture of Steve, "dressed in a green tablecloth, a cardboard crown on his head like the one on the Statue of Liberty . . . his hand aloft . . . but instead of a torch, there was a bottle of Budweiser, with an attached note, 'Give me your tired, your hungry Budweiser assignments, and I'll . . .'"

Steve got a job, and when Wally went to the president to request a budget for hiring Steve, the president gladly broke the rules and allocated the dollars.

Steve demonstrated many of the principles of the outstanding job searcher:

- He did outstanding research on the company he was targeting, not only about the company but about the person.
- He used a referral network to get the appointment.
- He stated that he wasn't just looking for a job but had very specific reasons why he wanted to work for Wally.
- He demonstrated creativity in bringing the bag full of items that represented Wally's accounts and relating them to his own life.
- He demonstrated professionalism when he showed his own ads, told which parts were his and which weren't, and showed some of his rejected ideas that he felt were good.
- He understood that a hiring freeze was not applicable if he had bottom-line value he could bring to the party.

- He realized that he would probably have to reconnect in order to demonstrate value and worth.
- He asked for feedback and then acted on it (the Polaroid picture).
- He was focused, and he followed through, took risks, and didn't let too much time go by between meetings.
- He was positive and proactive, stating that times would turn around and he wanted to be considered when they did.
- Steve saw this business of getting a job offer as one of being "in process." He took the initiative and responsibility to make it obvious that he could bring value to the bottom line— obvious that they needed him.

Have we succeeded in reframing you about the process of connecting? Do you feel less intimidated about job interviews? Can you picture ways in which you can actually have fun in the process? Now's the time to recall all the successful interactions and conversations that you've had in the course of your career. We encourage you to experience your connecting meetings with the same level of confidence and authenticity.

7

Your Career Dimensions
On Receiving No's, Maybe's, and Yes's—
And the Culmination of Your
Job Search

Joyce Sparks had been assistant director of career planning and placement at a midwestern university. In applying for director of career planning at another university, she submitted a strong cover letter and résumé, articles she had written for the local paper and for the career development association in which she was an elected board member, and outstanding letters of recommendation from former employers and others who knew her work. Because of her excellent experience and credentials, she believed that she had a good shot at the job.

Several weeks after the closing deadline, she received a call from a member of the university search committee to inform her that she had been selected with five other candidates, out of more than seventy applicants, to interview for the job. The interviewing process would consist of her meeting with her potential boss and another member of the search committee prior to coming to an interview with the rest of the committee.

Since she had more than a week before the interviews were to be held, Joyce prepared for them by compiling a five-page document that she planned to take with her when she met with her interviewers. Since she had been told that she would be interviewed by a total of eight people, Joyce prepared copies of her document for each person and enclosed them in clear plastic report folders with multicolored spines.

The first three pages outlined her preliminary ideas for contributions she planned to make to each area of the job if she were hired. The last two pages outlined capabilities and skills she had, with examples of how each would enhance her ability to excel in the job if she were offered the job.

Joyce believed that her interviews went well, although in an effort to speed through the six candidates, the two interviewers had given her only thirty-five minutes in the first interview. In the second, with five members of the search committee, she'd had an hour. At the second interview, one person had been absent, so the meeting had been taped for later listening.

Joyce was asked to respond to the same questions the other candidates had been asked. Not much time remained for her to ask her own questions, but she was glad that she was able to leave a copy of her document behind with each of the people reviewing her candidacy, to distinguish herself from the others.

She wrote a thoughtful and energetic thank-you letter, addressed to the chairperson of the search committee, adding comments about areas she felt were not adequately covered in the interviews. Joyce was confident that she had done an outstanding job throughout the interviewing process. She anticipated that none of the other candidates had been creative enough to go to the lengths she had, especially in preparing her "Proposal of Preliminary Ideas."

No more than a week later, Joyce received a telephone call from the chairperson of the search committee, telling her that another candidate had been selected instead of her. When she asked who it was, he told her it was an internal candidate. Still in shock, she requested an interview with the chairperson so that he could give her feedback about her presentation. She told him it would be helpful for future interviewing situations. He agreed to meet her a little more than a week later.

In the meeting, the chairperson made it clear that this feedback would include only his impressions, because the search committee had agreed to keep its proceedings confidential. He then went on to tell her that there were only two areas of concern that he had. On the whole he thought she clearly could have handled the duties of the position. He stated that he felt this was true as well for three of the other candidates. In his opinion, only one of the five people who had interviewed had not been qualified to the job.

His problems with her were that he thought that she was *too* energetic and a bit overpowering. She may have been able to get along with faculty, but he thought that alumni who felt more comfortable with people who were more "laid back" would have trouble relating with her. Secondly, he actually found her to be *too* organized.

Trying not to respond defensively, Joyce explained that she thought her style would be helpful to the students as well as in interacting with recruiters on and off campus. She also stated that she had presented her materials as thoroughly as possible so that they would have a clear picture of her skills, experience, and ideas for future programming.

Joyce was glad she had taken the time and had the nerve to follow up with this meeting. She discovered that not having been selected had more to do with style than anything else. Had she taken the position, she might not have been appreciated, might have been asked to conform to a laid-back posture that was foreign to her. Interestingly enough, through this meeting she solidified her relationship with the chairperson, who said he would be willing to refer her to colleagues at other universities as she continued her search.

Surprisingly, she heard little here that suggested that she conduct herself differently in future interviews. Rather than spend time imagining negatives that had no merit, she was able to put this situation completely behind her and continue her search.

If you're doing a thorough and effective job search, you should be collecting a hatful of no's and on your way to yes's. You'll be experiencing your share of rejections. People will not be hiring you because they think you are overqualified (a polite way of saying they don't know what to do with you and an indication that you may be communicating with a person at the wrong level in the organization) or underqualified (perhaps you weren't able to convince them of your unproven talents); because you were beat out by an internal candidate (you may never learn about this); because they thought you wouldn't be satisfied with the salary they were offering (but they never asked you directly); or because they believed the position would not be challenging enough for you (as if they would know).

Yet when you never hear a response after sending a well-conceived cover letter and résumé to a box number in the *Wall Street Journal,* or better yet, received a rejection letter in reply to your résumé, you may be tempted to think that they are rejecting *you.* You worry, "Maybe I'll never be hired! I'll never work again."

The real issue is that an integral part of the process of a job search or selling any product is rejection. It's built in. As a matter of fact, Tom Jackson, author of *Guerrilla Tactics in the Job Market* (Bantam Books, 1978), suggests that a job searcher will receive *twenty* no's before receiving a yes. Jackson tells his readers to type out a sheet of a hundred "NO"s and hang it over their work area. Every time a searcher gets a turn-down or refusal, he is to mark off a "NO" on the sheet. The goal is to cross out ten "NO"s a week.

Salespersons know that "no" is to be expected on the way to "yes." Baseball players know that batting averages include balls hit as well as balls missed. A batting average of .300, meaning three hits for every ten times at bat, translates into hitting the ball only 30 percent of the time.

Writers know that often their manuscripts are going to be turned down by many publishers before they are accepted. Some famous writers have been turned down as many as two hundred times.

Expect to be turned down along the way, being pleasantly surprised when you're not. One client of ours was turned down twenty times at a major company for which he was eager to work. As each of the twenty doors he came through closed behind him, he undauntingly tried another, until the twenty-first worked and he was finally hired.

What Are Your Compensation Goals?

It's bound to happen—even very early in your job search. You're at an exploratory meeting, and the first question you are asked is the inevitable, "So what kind of salary are you looking for?" They definitely *mean* well, because in their mind they are establishing parameters to help guide their thinking. They believe they can help you better if they have that information. And at first you may be inclined to agree with them.

However, it is preferable *not* to give out any information about your specific earnings expectations too early in the game, unless you are talking directly to a recruiter. It is better to focus on what you are capable of doing, what kind of position you are targeting, what problems you can help solve, what is going on out there in their company or industry, what possibilities the two of you can cook up together. When asked about salary goals, you can say something like, "The kind of contribution that I can make is more significant to me than the salary, at this point in my search." Or "Would you mind if we put our heads together and brainstorm about possibilities, without any restrictions getting in our way about what it might be worth?" Or "I don't want to rule out any possibilities at this stage." Or "Obviously, what I would want to be paid would have to be congruent with the structure and hierarchy of this company [or industry], and I'd want to be able to justify any salary I was offered by relating it to the bottom line."

But let's say your interviewer is persistent, and you cannot gracefully sidestep the entire discussion of money. You have tried the "let's put talk about dollars on the back burner, if you don't mind, since I don't want to rule out any possibilities too early in the game" approach, and it hasn't worked. Your next strategy should be to ask a question in response to the question you are asked.

For example, "What are you looking for in terms of dollars?" could be responded to with a question, "What do you believe the salary range would be for a design engineer in a company like this?" Or you could say, "I am really glad you asked. I've been wondering what your perspective—since you're really knowledgeable about this industry—would be on potential earnings for a sales manager." You might be able to steer the conversation away from you and learn something valuable in the process.

If you try the questions, and you still feel backed into a corner, you can talk in *ranges* of what you are targeting rather than answer any specific questions about your previous earnings history. So in response to "What was your previous salary?" you can say, "I am targeting positions in the $45,000 to $65,000 range, depending on the level of contribution." No need to go into more detail; people are used to thinking in terms of ranges. Companies often make offers out of a particular range they feel is appropriate for a position. Often there is some latitude about where you would fall within that range, depending on your experience, education, and negotiating ability. If you are in a much higher range, say over $100,000, it is even more acceptable to talk in large variances. You could say, "The range I am targeting is from $100,000 to $170,000." Due to the enormous importance of stock options, bonuses, and other perks, which often match or exceed actual salary at this level, such a range is entirely logical.

If you happen to be in a job interview, where salary is brought up early in the game to test whether you would be interested, and a number is stated that is way below your expectations, it is *still* better not to respond negatively. You *never* know what will happen. We've had clients listen openly to opportunities, go home and think creatively about what they could bring to the job that would enlarge it and enhance its importance, and then see the job actually jump to significantly higher levels of compensation later on in the dialogue process. If asked a direct question about whether "you'd be willing to take a job as a corporate litigation attorney at $55,000," you can say honestly that it is below your target range, but you're still interested in talking. And then you can proceed to look for ways to make yourself invaluable, to prove that you would be worth more and to look for ways to negotiate that salary up.

Ultimately your goal is to *defer* specific conversation about compensation until some sense of your worth to the organization is known, until you have had a number of meetings with a potential employer and have a clear sense of what you could do for them. The longer the process, the more chance that you can bridge the gap between your expectations and their perception of your value.

For example, if you are a controller who has sidestepped the issue of salary and has had several meetings with the financial vice president and the company president—and they really like you—your negotiating power will go up. There will be reluctance to start the interviewing process again with others, a process which in itself is time-consuming and expensive. It could be entirely possible for a $35,000 position in a small company to become a $43,000 position, in preference to beginning the interviewing process all over again. It is important not to allow yourself to become disappointed about apparently limited earnings possibilities too early in the game, before thinking of creative ways of impacting the offer.

The one exception to talking about salary and compensation expectations up front is when talking with a recruiter. He or she will want to know what your previous total package was and the current range you are targeting. When talking about ranges, you can say that you are targeting positions in the $50,000 to $85,000 range, depending on salary and stock option possibilities. If an employer is thinking about $50,000 as the top of the range, you can be considered. And if he is thinking of $85,000 as the bottom of his range, you can still be in the game. In other words, you try to position your range so that some employers will "reach down" to pull you into a range, and others will "reach up" to have a chance at hiring you.

It's best to be very direct with recruiters, who have certain boundaries over which they will not step. For example, if they are searching for a facilities manager for a major corporation, and you previously held that position at a small college, they might or might not consider you for the position.

They might make some allowance for your moving from academia to the profit sector, but they probably would not recommend you for a $75,000 job if your previous salary was $40,000. It doesn't mean you couldn't handle it or that it wouldn't be possible for you to secure a job with that much of a salary shift. It does mean that it probably will *not* happen through a recruiter, who is unlikely to stick his or her neck out to recommend you over other candidates.

What Are You Worth?

When you are out of a job, you will undoubtedly begin to question your own worth. Since your job is so intimately connected with your identity, it may be easy for you to lose sight of what you *are* indeed worth to another organization. Just because you are not employed right now does *not* mean that you are not worth a tremendous amount once you find the right fit, the right place to make a contribution.

Now is the time for you to do some research and check out what the positions you are targeting are worth in your field, in a particular market, with your unique blend of education and experience. Even if you are planning to replicate your previous job, now is the time to check and see whether you have been paid in accordance with industry salary surveys. If you are shifting from a sales manager in a corporation to a director of a not-for-profit foundation, it would be crucial for you to research what directors of not-for-profits generally are paid in the geographic location you are targeting.

If you are shifting your career from a corporate position to academia, or from an entrepreneurial organization to a not-for-profit, you may discover that a salary cut will be inevitable. But if you are creative, you can negotiate for time to do consulting, more vacation, paid seminars, trips to professional association meetings, and other perks that might adequately compensate for the lack of dollars.

After you have determined what scenarios you are planning to target, do some research on salary ranges. Ask everyone with whom you are networking, "I wonder if you would share with me what the salary range is for someone in a position at this level in an organization like this." Notice, you are asking for ranges. You are not asking them what they themselves are being paid. Most people will be very comfortable in providing you with this information.

Another good source of compensation information is through any personnel director who has continuing access to industry surveys. Or you can tap into your network of executive-compensation consultants who regularly survey changes in compensation levels. Companies need this information to make sure they are competitive in what they are paying new hires as well as long-time employees. And at least having this information can give you a place to start in your thinking about your worth in the marketplace.

But will you have any leverage? Can you *really* negotiate an offer when you are, after all, out of a job? Absolutely, and we'll talk about how to increase your chances by generating more than one offer at a time. In the best of situations, a job searcher has a couple of possibilities that are being considered at the same time. This gives him the opportunity to compare offers as well as to negotiate up an offer from someone who is willing to compete for his talents.

What Is Negotiation?

Negotiation is an interactive process in which you and your prospective employer shape the entire job package you are offered. In fact, you are actually negotiating from the very beginning of your job search—from the very first contact you have with a potential employer.

Negotiation includes how you look, what you communicate, how obvious your research has been, any initiative you have demonstrated, your level of persistence and resourcefulness, whether your creativity has surfaced, how clearly you have presented yourself, whether you have excelled at projecting yourself into their organization.

If your first contact was your résumé, then you want your résumé to reflect class, to reflect the level of job you are targeting. If you personally preceded your résumé, then your first impression, including how well you are dressed, must reflect the level of the position you are targeting. How smoothly you handle initial questions about compensation goals will become important—as a reflection of your negotiation ability.

There is an interesting phenomenon that occurs upon searching for a position. It is necessary to reflect, by the way you are dressed, the level of compensation you are targeting. So if you are shifting from not-for-profit to profit, now may be the time to invest in a couple of expensive suits. You are more likely to be paid what you are worth if you reflect that image from the beginning.

You might be thinking that it will be impossible to make the same salary as you were making before you lost your job. Outplacement companies nationwide report that, with an excellent job-search campaign, fired individuals are usually able to replicate their previous salary—and often increase it by 10 to 20 percent. As a matter of fact, it is often easier to get paid a salary congruent with your previous one than even to be seriously considered for a job at significantly less than what you were being paid. There is tremendous reluctance to hire someone at a lower salary than he or she made previously, simply because it is feared that this would be a stop-gap job for the person, who would be unhappy and would be out looking for another job that *would* match previous compensation.

Employers would not be suspicious if your career shift is intentional and you have good reasons why you are willing to accept a different salary range. For example, if you are shifting from business to academia, or from finance to community relations or training, you could make a case for having seriously considered what these changes will mean in terms of compensation. You're going in with your eyes open, and the employer will probably understand.

We worked with an environmental engineering consultant who decided to redirect his career to teaching children about the environment, either in school or camp settings. Obviously he would have to be prepared for a salary cut, and he encountered no resistance from potential employers in this area. He was actually able to match his consulting salary by combining his nine-month teaching salary with a two-month summer camp directorship.

In *Getting to Yes,* subtitled *Negotiating Agreement Without Giving In,* by Roger Fisher and William Ury of the Harvard Negotiation Project (Penguin Books, 1983), the reader is encouraged to participate in an alternative to "hard" or "soft" negotiation, engaging instead in what the authors call "principled negotiation." In principled negotiation, issues are decided on their merits rather than through a haggling process focused on what each side says it will and won't do. They suggest you look together for mutual gains and obtain what you are entitled to as a result of an open and fair dialogue.

Too often job searchers fear the negotiation process and get amnesia about what they actually know about the negotiation process. We have seen individuals experienced in mergers and acquisitions actually "forget" to negotiate when it comes to themselves. And if they do "forget" or decide not to negotiate, they take the chance of diminishing themselves in the eyes of the potential employer, who expects to see in action what he has been told about the job searcher's talents.

When you get to the negotiation stages, which should be toward the end of the interviewing process, after they have decided they want to hire you, picture yourself on a neutral mountain sitting across from each other in easy chairs, with a coffee table in between on which to set your coffee or tea. The scenery is beautiful, peaceful, calm. You are not among enemies, but among future colleagues and friends.

Give the negotiation process the same amount of careful attention you have given preceding sections of the interviewing process. Don't rush through it. Don't assume it has to be over in fifteen minutes. The higher up the job, the more attention you'll want to give to this process, since more benefits and perks are offered at the upper end of the spectrum. Assume that you *will* have some latitude to affect the offer—in terms of salary, perks, and other benefits.

Always Go for the Offer

If there is one strong belief that we hold, it is that you should always go for the offer, always take the position that you are *seriously* interested in an opportunity and are willing to listen to anything. If you are ambivalent because it appears that the job will be too low level, have the wrong salary or title, be a dead-end opportunity, or will require you to relocate and you really don't want to, you might have a tendency to sabotage what *could* turn into a wonderful opportunity that you *might* like.

A scientist who was targeting consulting companies received an offer to go interview at a company in a city that she would "never consider moving to," so she didn't want to "take advantage of them" by accepting their offer to be flown in for an interview. She was convinced she did not want to move, having recently refinished her enormous home and private lab space within it. She was equally as well convinced that this city where the consulting company was based would be too cold, and she wanted to stay in a warm climate.

We asked her if she was 100 percent sure she would not accept the position, under any circumstances. She said there was a 2 percent chance she would consider it—and so decided to go and test the waters. She was enamored with the young, entrepreneurial consulting company, staffed by a high-energy, brilliant group of scientists. She had never before encountered that level of commitment and intelligence in a small staff, and it was enough to convince her that she *would* consider a position there. She went for an offer. The irony of this story is that the company hired her *and* allowed her to remain in her home town, traveling throughout the country to do her consulting work and coming to corporate headquarters for a few days each month.

If she had not gone for the interview and had not proceeded with the process to the point of getting an offer, she would have never known what she had missed.

There is something magic that happens when you actually get an offer. You really do not know how you will feel about an offer until you have received one. It often feels different from what you expected. You now have an actual picture of what your role would be in this company. You are wanted as an employee, and that feels really good. You put the offer in your pocket, and you then have more leverage with your other targets. You thought you were projecting yourself into the company prior to the offer, but after receiving one, it feels different. Sometimes it feels a lot more exciting. Other times it will be clear that you were right after all—it is not the place for you. But getting the offer is important and will allow you to get some closure during this otherwise open-ended job-search process.

So go for the offer, and put it in your pocket. If you are offered a position, even if you are ambivalent about whether you want it, go ahead and negotiate the salary and perks. Explore what would make this opportunity really attractive to you. You might decide to defer the compensation negotiation process until you have decided whether you will accept it for the right price. The only problem with waiting to negotiate later is that the very package you negotiate *could* influence you to accept or reject an offer.

It is wise to say, "I appreciate the offer. I am very flattered that you see me as a good fit for your company, and I feel certain that I could make a major contribution to your strategic goals. I need to give this offer some very careful thought, since this is a very important decision for me. How about if I get back to you by the end of the week?" Or you can say, "I have no doubts at all about the job and the reporting structure. I would look forward to having an opportunity to work for you. Now I would like to speak with a few others in the division just to get a broader sense of the company culture—and to make sure it is as good a fit as it seems to be." In this way you can buy some time, learn more, investigate further, and have time to see if any of your other immediate targets are about to break.

The Negotiation

When you arrive at the actual moment of negotiation you should be fairly clear that they want you. It is important to have them state a salary or a range, rather than your stating anything specific at first. In response to "So what would it take to get you, Jack?" you would respond, "I would be interested in hearing what your range is for this position. Obviously I would want to be paid what I am worth—and in line with others at this level in your company. I have done some investigation and do have a sense of what a systems analyst would be paid in this industry, but of course I would be open to any discussion. What did you have in mind?"

After you have been told a compensation number or range, then you begin to negotiate by asking numerous questions about how they arrived at that number, how it fits within the range of others at that level, why they chose that number as opposed to a different one. It is important to know where they are coming from in order to negotiate that number up.

- "We chose this salary range because it is the midpoint of the salaries we pay to design engineers." (Later you can counter with "But I see myself operating way above the midpoint—and would like to share the reasons why.")
- "We chose this salary because it is five thousand dollars more than your previous salary—and we thought it was fair." (Is it fair if you will be paid significantly less than others at your level? Could you refocus the conversation on level of contribution and explain that according to salary surveys your salary

in a hospital setting is equal to a 20 percent higher salary in a corporate setting, thus making a case for placing you in a more appropriate range?)

- "We don't place executives at this level on the stock option track." (Could you strategize to retitle the position so that you could be eligible for a company car and other more senior executive benefits?)
- "We really want you for this position and will offer you five thousand dollars more than your previous one." (All well and good, but you are considering relocating to California, and you'll need a lot more than that just to replicate your current standard of living. Can you share what you have discovered upon researching standard-of-living costs between the Mid-

west and the West Coast? Can you negotiate for a much higher salary than what you were making because it is still in line with industry standards?)

What Can You Negotiate For?

James R. Baehler, author of *Book of Perks,* has written an outstanding book which can provide you with a detailed look at specific perks for which you can negotiate.

Salary

Baehler talks about using your network to identify pay scales for the job you are targeting, in the appropriate industry and in your geographical location. The compensation of principal officers to public corporations are disclosed in proxy statements and 10K reports, which must be filed with the Securities and Exchange Commission as addenda to their annual reports. Other ways to secure cash include asking for a signing bonus (find out if it has ever been done in this company), an annual performance bonus (find out if this company has such a plan), a severance settlement and outplacement assistance (if there is a takeover or buy-out and you find yourself in this situation again sooner than you expected).

You can also negotiate for the right to do consulting or writing on your own time and to retain ownership of anything written outside work. (Where once this approach was not possible—since companies expected total devotion from their employees—times have changed. Many people are looking for ways to diversify their earnings and decrease their reliance on the paycheck coming from only one source.)

According to Baehler, a study done by the American Management Association of 1,451 companies found that 61 percent had a bonus or incentive plan of some kind, with bonuses in some situations averaging 36.1 percent of base salaries. That figure however is somewhat distorted by the enormous bonuses paid to CEOs, and in actuality the median of most bonuses would be between 15 and 20 percent.

Stock Options

In the April 24, 1989, *Wall Street Journal,* in an article entitled "A Great Leap Forward for Executive Pay," it was stated that in a Towers, Perrin study of forty of the top one hundred U.S. companies, salaries and bonuses in general (not counting stock options) were up sharply in 1988. But the article goes on to discuss that the really big gains in compensation have come from the exercise of stock options, which give the individual holding the options an opportunity to buy shares at a set price—sometime in the future. Quoting Pearl Meyer, president of Pearl Meyer & Partners, a compensation consulting firm, the article says, "Many stock-option grants are so large that even a small increase in stock price could yield sizable payouts. . . . The average size of stock-option grants went up 15% in 1988 from 1987. The average public company is now setting aside 1% of its stock a year to give to upper management, usually a group of no more than 50 people."

The reason stock options have become so popular is that they link company performance to executive compensation. The reason your research prior to negotiating for a job is so important is that you'll want to find out whether you could be positioned so that you could take advantage of stock options. It certainly would be worth some strategizing.

Relocation Benefits

Getting an offer in another city definitely has its own set of complications. Baehler states that it cost an average of $40,000 in the early 1980s to move a family of four a thousand miles. Baehler recommends that you request a minimum of three visits by you and your spouse to the new location to find a new home—and adequate support if you are required to find temporary housing.

You'll want to investigate cost-of-living differences in the new location. If you are leaving a $350-per-month mortgage to acquire a $2,000-per-month mortgage in a new location, what will happen to your standard of living, even with a good salary increase? Can you negotiate the company picking up a mortgage differential for a few years or even a monthly housing subsidy to offset the enormous increase in housing costs?

"Peace of Mind" Perks

Baehler states that you need not be bound by the terms of the company pension plan, even if you are not eligible at first. He suggests ways around the ineligibility problem, including asking the company to compute the lost benefits and paying that amount into your IRA account. He recommends you pay close attention to life insurance. In a 1981 survey of 731 companies done by the AMA, 47 percent provided additional life insurance to their executives. Also investigate wellness benefits, health club memberships, additional training and education, financial and legal consultation, and disability benefits.

Tax Benefits

Even though the benefits of a company car are diminished some because of the changes of tax laws, it is still an enormous advantage to be offered a company car. In a survey quoted by Baehler, 28.7 percent of middle managers were provided additional medical coverage above and beyond the standard plan. It is certainly worth checking.

"The Good Life"

Baehler includes in this category a discussion of club memberships, travel, spouse's travel, airline clubs, extra vacation time, and sabbaticals.

In an article in the March 27, 1989, issue of *Fortune* magazine,

John Sculley talks about his recent sabbatical of nine weeks, during which he regenerated his energy and enthusiasm and luxuriated in time to think, plan, reevaluate, and learn something new. He even took up photography as a novice, which gave him new insight into resistance others may have to computers.

Apple has a policy that after five years of employment with the company, an employee is eligible for a six-week sabbatical. Sculley tacked on his three-week vacation—and is very enthusiastic about his experience.

Image and Status

Here, Baehler discusses office space, private secretaries, executive-dining-room privileges, travel on the company jet, company-paid parking space, even a chauffeured limousine and access to company vacation homes.

We'll add here a reminder to think creatively about position titles. If someone wants to hire you, but can't justify the salary you want, perhaps the two of you can come up with a different title that won't alienate anyone else in the company but will allow you to be at the level you are targeting.

Baehler's message throughout his wonderful book is that if you don't ask, you won't get. There's one thing we know from experience: there is practically no leverage after you have accepted a position. And that is essentially why you don't want to accept an offer on the spot—even after you have done some negotiating. It is important to go home, sleep on it, think through what will really make you happy, and have one last shot at what you might have forgotten to address.

Getting an Offer Letter

It is a good idea to ask for an offer in writing, following the negotiation. It is not at all uncommon for a company to put an offer in writing and send it to the potential employee prior to acceptance.

How you ask for the offer letter may be crucial. You are *not* suspicious. You are *not* doubting their integrity. You are not concerned that anyone will go back on their word.

Rather you want to have everything reviewed in writing, so that you can make sure that *you* have not forgotten to address something. You want to be careful and thoughtful about this important decision, and it is a good protection against thinking you agreed on something that was in fact not agreed upon.

If you sense some resistance from them to putting it in writing, then you can offer to do so. "How about if I just put down in writing what we have agreed upon, and send you over a copy so that we can have our signals straight? Then, if you'll just initial it, we'll be sure we're on the same wavelength." This approach can, in addition, buy you some time to check back with other possible opportunities that might be about to break.

There are many legal reasons why a company might be reluctant to put an offer in writing—what with wrongful-discharge lawsuits becoming so common. But what you want is some assurance that this offer will not evaporate if, for example, the person hiring you decides to accept a position elsewhere, even prior to your starting employment. It has happened often enough.

Why Are They So Slow?

When you are in a job search, sometimes time seems to stand still. You have done everything but stand on your head, and it seems like they are *really* interested in you. They've expressed direct interest, but an offer has not yet been extended. Your strategy should be to continue to reconnect, as if they still need *more* information about you, enough to get them over the critical mass of information and trust necessary to make the job offer. You continue to think of things to send, reasons for meetings, ideas to share. While you are focused on your job search, they are involved in the day-to-day activities of running a business or doing their jobs, and they are not experiencing the same degree of urgency as you are.

While they are in the process of considering whether to hire you—that's when you go out and work hard to bring some of the other possibilities you have uncovered to fruition. You will have the strongest negotiating power when it gets to the actual offer time if you have *more than one offer*. Having more than one offer can help compensate for being out of a job. When you are negotiating from the strength of having a job, you have leverage. Having more than one hard-core possibility will give you more leverage than you would have otherwise.

Believe it or not, you could actually even view their slow pace as being in your best interest, since it allows you to position yourself for a stronger negotiating stance.

Juggling Possibilities

How do you buy yourself time, so that one offer can be held in abeyance while you consider another carefully? It is quite difficult, since once a company extends an offer, they are not usually very patient. They usually want an answer, and often, even if they have kept you dangling for three months, they want your answer yesterday.

One way to buy yourself time is to ask for the offer letter. Another is to state that you now would like the time to talk to a few more people, to spend some time in the field with the sales manager, or in the plant with the systems engineers, in order to make sure that this is the right decision for you. You say it *very* positively, with all kinds of anticipation and enthusiasm about your confidence that you will join the company. But it does buy you some time, while you consider other options, if the company is open to this kind of personal investigation.

Not all companies are open or will respond positively to this kind of curiosity. The smaller, more entrepreneurial organizations may be more open to this kind of approach. But we have not yet seen this approach backfire when done correctly. Permission is not always given, but we have not seen offers withdrawn because of such a request.

Risk Factors of
Negotiating

We would be remiss if we didn't admit that there is always a risk that when you negotiate you will alienate a potential employer. It has been our experience that for the most part, deciding to negotiate has been more of an asset than a liability.

But there have been occasions where even just *asking* a question has alienated a potential employer to such a degree that the offer has been withdrawn. The fear that this potential employee would be dissatisfied, would be a troublemaker, would never really be happy at that company may not go away. So we don't want you to think we're naive. It *is* a risk to negotiate. It is also a risk not to, since you are negotiating for your very livelihood and will have to live with the results for quite a while.

Ultimately you'll have to be the judge, and it will depend on how marketable you feel after you design a strong job search, how many possibilities you are able to uncover, what your personal financial situation is, and how much of a risk taker you are.

When a "No" Can Lead to a "Yes"

If you are rejected, we want to urge you to think carefully about the reasons why—and even evaluate whether you want to approach the potential employer again. And the same can be true for working through recruiters, who may initially consider you for a position and then reject you as "missing" certain qualifications. It is worth a shot to ask questions about the issues that eliminated you from the race and address your qualifications, if you think you have been eliminated unfairly.

One of our clients was told by a recruiter that he would be one of three interviewed for a senior executive position in a health-care organization but later was told by the recruiter that his references had been checked and he had been eliminated as a candidate at this time. When the client asked questions as to reasons why, he discovered that his management style was in question, and he wanted an opportunity to clarify it to the recruiter. It turned out that the recruiter had checked with several people whose names had not been given out by our client as references (but who were well known in the industry), and those people had actually gotten the client confused with someone else.

Actually, his management style matched *exactly* what the employer was looking for. He got his interview, due to his persistence and his refusal to accept rejection without explanation.

Often a no can lead to a yes a few months or a couple of years later, when there is a reorganization or restructuring or when a job more congruent with your strengths might surface. That is why it is essential to reconnect with each of those who seriously considered you for a job but rejected you in the end. They can be helpful in giving you information for your continued search. And they might very well recruit you at some later time for a different job— especially if they feel comfortable about the way in which you reacted to rejection. You'd be surprised at the number of stories we have heard from former clients about job opportunities that popped up a few months to even a few years later, as a result of handling these rejections with finesse.

One final note about those doing the rejecting. They usually struggle a great deal prior to making a choice, and it is not an easy process for them to go through. In a sense their reputation is on the line, since they are responsible for making good hires. Often these can become your *best* supporters in the continuation of your job search. No kidding. They obviously were impressed enough to "almost" hire you. You *did* beat out many other contenders. You *are* obviously talented, or they would not have spent so much time with you in the first place.

Add them to your networking process, as Joyce, the assistant director of career planning and placement mentioned earlier in the chapter, decided to do. Go back to them, talk about why you were screened out. And then ask for assistance in the continuation of your search. Ask for referral names. Even ask for phone calls of introduction if the vibes are right. You may be surprised at the results you'll attain from initiating such an encounter.

After You Accept an Offer, Who
Do You Reconnect With?

Everyone! The first communication, of course, should be a letter of acceptance, with all the agreed-upon stipulations, to your new boss. Include your personal thoughts about how positively you are looking forward to this professional relationship. Like the thank-you letters written after interviews, this is more than just courtesy. You want to provide a record for the future so that there will be clarity about the offer. Keep a copy of the letter.

A week or two after you have been in your job, you'll want to write a letter briefly describing your new situation and duties, to be sent out to everyone you have connected with during your search. This can include people you met with face-to-face and on the phone—anyone who has been instrumental in your process, as well as those who would want to know your whereabouts for the future.

Compiling this list and sending out a letter can help you in many ways. You will end up with a central listing of names and addresses. There may be people on this list that you will want to do business with or recruit for your company later on. Finally, when you are ready to conduct another search, possibly three to five years down the road, you will have the names and addresses of contacts and recruiters. Since recruiters love to maintain contact with talented people, knowing where to find you easily may persuade a recruiter or two to contact you when an interesting opportunity comes along. Having a list of your contacts, to which you can add names down the road, will prevent you from being unprepared. You'll have an insurance policy. You won't ever have to start a new search from scratch.

Networking for Life
with a Purpose

When you look back on all that you have gained through your job search, like most of our clients you will feel that you have much more than you had before you started. In addition to what you have learned about your potential through exploring your unique dimensions, and your increased knowledge from research you conducted and from keeping your antennae up, you will have developed a new network of professional colleagues and friends.

You'll realize that each of these new contacts will have enriched you in ways that you couldn't have imagined. Taking the opportunity to look back on your search is a good time to resolve to continue your networking and connecting with others, not at the rate you did throughout your search, of course, but with the goal of meeting at least several new people a month. In this way, you will remain current and on your toes. You'll have opportunities to give as well as take, helping others who perhaps are in the midst of their own job searches.

You will be networking with a purpose: to expand your horizons; to prevent yourself from developing narrow vision; to expand your knowledge base both inside and outside your immediate field of expertise; to every once in a while network toward a dream.

Burt was an effective, experienced controller whose company was dissolved without any warning, leaving him with the necessity of doing a job search. He generated a large number of alternatives and toward the end of his job search was confronted with a difficult dilemma. He was faced with whether to accept a good offer, which included an increase, financially, from what he had been earning at his previous position, or to turn this offer down and continue his job search with the idea of generating a more exciting opportunity.

The offer came after three months of intensive job searching and a couple of live opportunities that had excited him but had fallen through. He was, frankly, tired of looking for a job and ready to work in one.

Burt weighed the pros and cons of this new position. The pros included the facts that he would not have to move his young family, the position would be easy for him, the salary and perk package were ample and could provide him with considerable financial advantages.

The cons included the facts that the company was small and privately held (he was used to a large public corporation), the individual who ran the company knew very little about the financial end of a business, and there was a great deal to straighten out before the business could be fully and accurately evaluated regarding its real earnings. He would be somewhat isolated in his function, and the industry did not really excite him anymore.

In short, it was not the perfect job but was certainly adequate, at least for the short or medium term. He decided to accept the position, intending to do an excellent job, to remain for an indefinite period of time, and to continue with his networking in a much more measured manner.

Taking the job, he had the additional benefit of not being out of a job and no longer having to deal with the feelings of insecurity that he experienced throughout his job search. He joined a couple of professional organizations but settled down to do his job well and to make a significant contribution to this organization.

About a year and a half later, Burt received a telephone call from a friend who had worked with him at his previous position and who had been contacted by a search firm. The recruiter was looking for a high-level financial person to assist a company in readying itself to go public. Burt's friend was not interested in the position and referred the call to him, even though he had no idea whether Burt would consider making a change again so soon.

In keeping with his new open attitude, Burt flew to the East Coast and interviewed with the president of this organization. He sufficiently impressed them, because an offer that he could not refuse followed, as well as the surprising information that the company was relocating to his hometown, and he would not even have to relocate. His new position offered significant financial gains, as well as an opportunity for stock options in the company after it went public.

Burt anticipates that this new position will satisfy a great many of his needs and intends to work hard to justify his excellent financial package of salary plus perks. But he stated unequivocally that he will continue networking, meeting with interesting people, learning of other options there may be for him in the future.

Burt will never again be caught unprepared, though he may indeed be caught unaware or by surprise when his company is gobbled up by a larger institution and he finds himself in a job-search mode once again. It does not depress him to think of that happening. He feels empowered to conduct a good job search if necessary and has adopted an open-ended approach to planning his career.

And this is our hope for you. Sometime in the near future, you will be looking back on this episode in your life with the same resolve and clarity that Burt has. As you continue to network throughout the rest of your career, you can remember the words of Robert Muller, whose opening lines of poetry are found in the beginning of *The Networking Book: People Connecting with People* (Routlege, Chapman and Hally, 1986) by Jessica Lipnack and Jeffrey Stamps:

> Decide to network
> Use every letter you write
> Every conversation you have
> Every meeting you attend
> To express your fundamental beliefs and dreams
> Affirm to others the vision of the world you want

In this way, you will raise your day-to-day consciousness about your work and how it integrates into your life. And you can even enjoy the process along the way. Networking could well become a lifelong habit. You'll wonder how you ever got along before without such purposeful connecting in your life. You may even begin to realize that losing your job just might have been one of the best things that has ever happened to you.